The Ecological Thought

The Ecological Thought

TIMOTHY MORTON

HARVARD UNIVERSITY PRESS
Cambridge, Massachusetts, and London, England

Copyright © 2010 by the President and Fellows of Harvard College
All rights reserved
Printed in the United States of America

First Harvard University Press paperback edition, 2012

Library of Congress Cataloging-in-Publication Data

Morton, Timothy, 1968–
  The ecological thought / Timothy Morton.
    p. cm.
  Includes bibliographical references (p.   ) and index.
  ISBN 978-0-674-04920-8 (cloth : alk. paper)
  ISBN 978-0-674-06422-5 (pbk.)
  1. Ecology—Philosophy.   I. Title.
  QH540.5.M66 2010
  577.01—dc22

2009038804

For Claire

Contents

Acknowledgments

A big thank you to David Simpson, my distinguished colleague, David Robertson, and Margaret Ferguson, Chairs of the Department of English at the University of California, Davis: they've created a flourishing environment for me. I owe a debt of immense gratitude to Lindsay Waters at Harvard University Press, for believing in me. Lindsay gave inspiring and learned advice and transformed the last two years into the most pleasant and educational writing stint of my life. Thank you to Tsoknyi Rinpoche, who influences my thinking in ways too many to enumerate. And thank you to Gerardo Abboud, for taking a group to Tibet in Fall 2007.

Profound thanks are due to this book's two anonymous readers. I'm grateful to David Clark for having read a draft. Marjorie Levinson helped me clarify my thinking immensely. Dimitris Vardoulakis kindly commented on the manuscript. David Robertson likewise gave encouraging and valuable advice, and so did Vince Carducci. The project received generous support from UC Davis's Publication Assistance Fund.

Thanks to my graduate students, especially Andrew Hageman, Laura Hudson, Eric O'Brien, Chris Schaberg, Rachel Swinkin, and Clara Van Zanten. I'm grateful to the Association for the Study of Literature and the Environment (UK), and in particular to Greg Garrard and Tom Bristow for hosting their and my first videoconference keynote speech in July 2008, low on carbon and high on philosophical exchange; to the Centre for Research in the Arts, Social Sciences and Humanities at Cambridge

University, and in particular Benjamin Morris and Bradon Smith; to the International Association for Environmental Philosophy; Amy Greenstadt and the Portland Center for Public Humanities; Gerry Canavan and the *Polygraph* crew at Duke University; Deborah Elise White at Emory University; and Stephanie Lemenager at UC Santa Barbara. Thanks to Vince Carducci for inviting me to Cranbrook Academy of Art in Fall 2007. Thank you to Ann Greer for providing a home away from home in London in Spring 2008.

Thanks to Warner/Chappell, Alfred Publishing and the Richmond Organization, for granting permission to reproduce lyrics by Roger Waters for the Pink Floyd song "Echoes" from the album *Meddle* (EMI, 1971), in the epigraph for Chapter 2; © Copyright 1971 Warner/Chapell and the Richmond Organization (TRO-© Copyright 1971 (Renewed), 1976 (Renewed) Hampshire House Publishing Corp., New York, NY). Used by permission.

Thank you to my terrific research assistant, Sara Anderson. Thanks to Ron Broglio, Kurt Fosso, and Ashton Nichols, collaborators on a stimulating Romantic Circles blog on ecocriticism; and to readers of my blog ecologywithoutnature.blogspot.com. Thank you, too, Ruth Abbott, Shahidha Bari, Jeremy Braddock, Nathan Brown, Patrick Curry, John Davie, Fran Dolan, Elizabeth Fay, Svein Hatlevik, Caspar Henderson, Srecko Horvat, Douglas Kahn, Peter King, Claire Lamont, Mike Luthi, Glen Mazis, Jacob Metcalf, Colin Milburn, Jasmine Morton, Ava Neyer, Derek Parfit, Arkady Plotnitsky, Kate Rigby, Michael Rossington, Scott Shershow, Jane Stabler, Ted Toadvine, Robert Unger, Karen Weisman, Patricia Yaeger, Michael Ziser, and Slavoj Žižek. A heartfelt thank you to my wife, Kate, who as ever thought, walked, and talked this project through with me. All the errors herein are my responsibility alone.

I dedicate this book to my daughter Claire. Thinking about her takes me into realms of the unspeakable, just like the ecological thought. They are realms of unspeakable love.

Infinity overflows the thought that thinks it

Emmanuel Levinas

The Ecological Thought

Introduction: Critical Thinking

The ecological crisis we face is so obvious that it becomes easy—for some, strangely or frighteningly easy—to join the dots and see that everything is interconnected. This is *the ecological thought*. And the more we consider it, the more our world opens up.

We usually think of ecology as having to do with science and social policy. But as the poet Percy Shelley said, regarding developments in science, "We want the creative faculty to imagine that which we know."[1] Ecology seems earthy, pedestrian. It's something to do with global warming, recycling, and solar power; something to do with quotidian relationships between humans and nonhumans. Sometimes we associate ecology with fervent beliefs that are often explicitly religious: the Animal Liberation Front or Earth First! To the extent that we don't yet have a truly ecological world, religion cries aloud in a green voice.[2] But what would an ecological society look like? What would an ecological mind think? What kinds of art would an ecologically minded person enjoy? All these questions have one thing in common: *the ecological thought*.

As the success of the 2008 Pixar masterpiece *Wall • E* demonstrated, the question is on everyone's mind: what is ecological awareness?[3] How do we restart Spaceship Earth with the pieces we have to hand? How do we move forward from the melancholy of a poisoned planet? *Wall • E* begins several hundred years into the future, with the depressing scene of a little garbage-compacting robot piling skyscraper-high towers of human detritus. There's something wrong with "his" software, something that manifests as an obsessive collecting. It looks like he's searching for some key to humanness among the Rubik's Cubes, the video of *Hello Dolly*, the tiny sprout in a flowerpot. *Wall • E* happily shows that the "broken" software, the mental disorder of the little robot, is the viral code that reboots Earth: this time around, we evolve from memes, not genes. Yet isn't his obsessive compulsion, so like a manifestation of grief (from where we sit in the cinema at least, spectators to future ruin), exactly our situation right now? How do we begin? Where do we go from here? Is that the sound of something calling us from within the grief—the sound of the ecological thought?

The ecological thought is a virus that infects all other areas of thinking. (Yet viruses, and virulence, are shunned in environmental ideology.) This book argues that ecology isn't just about global warming, recycling, and solar power—and also not just to do with everyday relationships between humans and nonhumans. It has to do with love, loss, despair, and compassion. It has to do with depression and psychosis. It has to do with capitalism and with what might exist after capitalism. It has to do with amazement, open-mindedness, and wonder. It has to do with doubt, confusion, and skepticism. It has to do with concepts of space and time. It has to do with delight, beauty, ugliness, disgust, irony, and pain. It has to do with consciousness and awareness. It has to do with ideology and critique. It has to do with reading and writing. It has to do with race, class, and gender. It has to do with sexuality. It has to do with ideas of self and the weird paradoxes of subjectivity. It has to do with society. It has to do with coexistence.

Like the shadow of an idea not yet fully thought, a shadow from the future (another wonderful phrase of Shelley's), the ecological thought creeps over other ideas until nowhere is left untouched by its dark presence.[4] Darwin trusted the theory of evolutionary impermanence so much that he was prepared to suspend his disbelief in continental permanence, although in his day there was no tectonic plate theory.[5] Such is the force of the ecological thought. As one philosopher put it (see this book's epigraph), "infinity overflows the thought that thinks it."[6]

You could think of *The Ecological Thought* as the prequel to my previous book, *Ecology without Nature*. What must I have been thinking in order to realize that in order to have "ecology," we have to let go of "nature"?[7] You can't make a prequel until you have made the "original" movie. In some strong sense, the ecological thought rigorously comes afterward—it is always to come, somewhere in the future. In its fullest scope, it *will have been thought* at some undefined future point. You find yourself caught in its tractor beam (it's like a mathematical "attractor"). You didn't mean to. You must have been thinking it all along. But you had no idea. The ecological thought sneaks up on you from the future, a picture of what will have had to be there, already, for "ecology without nature" to make sense.

Like archaeologists of the future, we must piece together what will have been thought. Ultimately, the ecological thought surpasses what passes for environmentalism. It thinks otherwise than small-minded, and big-minded, manipulation. It goes beyond thinking "How many other living beings must we kill in order to be around next winter?" It goes beyond "Whatever is, is right."[8] It goes beyond "Let it be, let it be."[9] It goes beyond self, Nature, and species. It goes beyond survival, Being, destiny, and essence. Yet like a virus, like the lowest of the lowest (are they even alive?), like the tiny macromolecules in our cells, in our very DNA, the ecological thought has been there all along.

Why "ecology without nature"? "Nature" fails to serve ecology well. I shall sometimes use a capital *N* to highlight its "unnatural" qualities, namely (but not limited to), hierarchy, authority, harmony, purity, neutrality, and mystery. Ecology can do without a concept of a something, a thing of some kind, "over yonder," called Nature. Yet thinking, including ecological thinking, has set up "Nature" as a reified thing in the distance, under the sidewalk, on the other side where the grass is always greener, preferably in the mountains, in the wild. One of the things that modern society has damaged, along with ecosystems and species and the global climate, is thinking. Like a dam, Nature contained thinking for a while, but in the current historical situation, thinking is about to spill over the edge.

Ecological thinking might be quite different from our assumptions about it. It isn't just to do with the sciences of ecology. Ecological thinking is to do with art, philosophy, literature, music, and culture. Ecological thinking has as much to do with the humanities wing of modern universities as with the sciences, and it also has to do with factories, transportation, architecture, and economics. Ecology includes all the ways we imagine how we live together. Ecology is profoundly about coexistence. Existence is always coexistence. No man is an island.[10] Human beings need each other as much as they need an environment. Human beings *are* each others' environment. Thinking ecologically isn't simply about nonhuman things. Ecology has to do with you and me.

Why call this book *The Ecological Thought?* Why not *An Ecological Thought* or *Some Ecological Thoughts?* Or more modestly, *Notes toward Ecological Thinking?* Or just *Ecological Thought?* Of course there are ecological thoughts. And this book has no monopoly on ecological thinking. But there is a particular kind of thinking that I call *the* ecological thought. It runs like a strand of DNA code through thousands of other kinds of thoughts. Moreover, the *form* of the ecological thought is at least as important as its *content*. It's not simply a matter of *what* you're thinking about. It's also a matter of *how* you think. Once you start to think the ecological thought, you can't unthink it: it's a sphincter—once it's open, there's no closing.

THE SCOPE OF THE DAMAGE

Modern economic structures have drastically affected the environment. Yet they have had an equally damaging effect on thinking itself. I don't mean that before now we thought ecologically and properly. The ecological thought in its full richness and depth was unavailable to nonmodern humans. Even now, on the brink—over the brink, indeed—of climate catastrophe, we're only just capable of glimpsing its magnitude and profundity. The modern age compels us to think big, in the words of the first chapter. Any thinking that avoids this "totality" is part of the problem. So we have to face it. Something about modern life has prevented us from thinking "totality" as big as we could. Now we can't help but think it. Totality looms like a giant skyscraper shadow into the flimsiest thought about, say, today's weather. We may need to think bigger than totality itself, if totality means something closed, something we can be sure of, something that remains the same. It might be harder to imagine four and a half billion years than abstract eternity. It might be harder to imagine evolution than to imagine abstract infinity. It's a little humiliating. This "concrete" infinity directly confronts us in the actuality of life on Earth. Facing it is one of the profound tasks to which the ecological thought summons us.

We've gotten it wrong so far—that's the truth of climate disruption and mass extinction. I don't advocate a return to premodern thinking. The ecological thought is modern. The paradox is that the modern era—let's say it began around the late eighteenth century—impeded its own access to the ecological thought, even though the ecological thought will have been one of its lasting legacies. As far as ecology goes, modernity spent the last two and a half centuries tilting at windmills. The ghost of "Nature," a brand new entity dressed up like a relic from a past age, haunted the modernity in which it was born.[11] This ghostly Nature inhibited the growth of the ecological thought. Only now, when contemporary capitalism and consumerism cover the entire Earth and reach deeply into its life forms, is it possible, ironically and at last, to let go of this nonexistent ghost. Exorcise is good for you, and human beings are past the point at which Nature is a help. Our continued survival, and therefore the survival of the planet we're now dominating beyond all doubt, depends on our thinking past Nature.

Modern thinkers had taken it for granted that the ghost of Nature, rattling its chains, would remind them of a time without industry, a time without "technology," as if we had never used flint or wheat. But in looking at the ghost of Nature, modern humans were looking in a mirror. In Nature, they saw the reflected, inverted image of their own age—and the grass is always greener on the other side. Nature was always "over yonder," alien and alienated.[12] Just like a reflection, we can never actually reach it and touch it and belong to it. Nature was an ideal image, a self-contained form suspended afar, shimmering and naked behind glass like an expensive painting. In the idea of pristine wilderness, we can make out the mirror image of private property: Keep off the Grass, Do Not Touch, Not for Sale. Nature was a special kind of private property, without an owner, exhibited in a specially constructed art gallery. The gallery was Nature itself, revealed through visual technology in the eighteenth century as "picturesque"—looking like a picture.[13] The "new and improved" version is art without an object, just an aura: the glow of value.[14] Nature isn't what it claims to be.

While we're on the subject of Nature and "new and improved" upgrades, this book makes a rigorous distinction between *environmentalism* and *ecology*. By the time you finish, you may feel that there are good reasons for advocating not just ecology without nature but also *ecology without environmentalism*.

In *Reflections on the Edge of Askja*, Pall Skulason tells us why we need Nature:

> To live, to be able to exist, the mind must connect itself with some kind of order. It must apprehend reality as an independent whole . . . and must bind itself in a stable fashion to certain features of what we call reality. It cannot bind itself to the ordinary world of everyday experience, except by taking it on faith that reality forms an objective whole, a whole which exists independently of the mind. The mind lives, and we live, in a relationship of faith with reality itself. This relationship is likewise one of confidence in a detached reality, a reality which is different and other than the mind. We live and exist in this relationship of confidence, which is always by its nature uncertain and insecure. . . . [This] relationship of confidence . . . is originally, and truly, always a relationship with reality as a natural totality: as Nature.[15]

It isn't hard to detect in this passage the violent, repetitive actions of someone desperate to restart a broken machine. Skulason cranks handles, attaches jumper cables, rolls it down a hill . . . it's not just what he says or even how he says it. It's the attitude with which he says it, the "subject position." From the tone of hope and fear, you can tell that the game is up and that he knows it. He is indulging in magical thinking: "If I just keep saying this in the right way, it'll be okay. Nature will exist." The desperation is legible in the sheer amount of writing. It goes on and on, waiting for something that never comes. It's Nature writing reduced to *Waiting for Godot:* "I must keep going. I can will Nature into existence, write it into the script." Skulason is trying to cheer us up in the middle of the slow motion disaster we're facing. The more he says, the worse it gets.

In the name of ecology, we must scrutinize Nature with all the suspicion a modern person can muster. Let the buyer beware. Nature has turned out to be a plastic knockoff of the real thing. As Emmanuel Levinas puts it in an astonishing passage that is among other things a passionate critique of deep ecology's favorite philosopher, Martin Heidegger, our concepts of "faceless generous mother nature" are based on "sedentary" agricultural societies with their idea of "possession." The myth of the faceless mother provides the very motivation for our exploitation of Earth, seen as "inexhaustible matter for things."[16] Wilderness areas are giant, abstract versions of the products hanging in mall windows. Even when we've tried to preserve an enclave of safety from the ravages of the modern age, we've been getting it all wrong, on a more profound level.

Can we get over our addiction to possession and the myth of the faceless mother? What is the real thing? We can get a sense of it, to be sure, though it will upgrade our ideas of "real" and "thing" to boot. Ecology shows us that all beings are connected. *The ecological thought* is the thinking of interconnectedness. The ecological thought is a thought about ecology, but it's also a thinking that is ecological. Thinking the ecological thought is part of an ecological project. The ecological thought doesn't just occur "in the mind." It's a practice and a process of becoming fully aware of how human beings are connected with other beings—animal, vegetable, or mineral. Ultimately, this includes thinking about democracy. What would a truly democratic encounter between truly equal beings look like, what would it be—can we even imagine it?

When we start looking, we find the ecological thought everywhere. This isn't surprising, since the ecological thought is interconnectedness in the fullest and deepest sense. Even Descartes' infamous "I think therefore I am" takes place in an environment, and this environment is present in the very text of the cogito. Descartes begins the *Meditations* by describing himself sitting by a fire, holding in his hand the paper on which he is writing.[17] Environmentalist thinking frequently condemns Cartesianism as a prototype of the dreaded dualism that separates mind and body, self and world, subject and object. Descartes is framed as environmental public enemy number one. The ecological thought insists that we're deeply connected even when we say we're not. Thinking itself is an ecological event. The kind of environmentalist ideology that wishes that we had never started to think—ruthlessly immediate, aggressively masculine, ruggedly anti-intellectual, afraid of humor and irony—is dubious at best. In fact, it's part of the problem. The constant assertion that we're "embedded" in a lifeworld is, paradoxically, a symptom of drastic separation.[18]

When we think the ecological thought, we encounter all kinds of beings that are not strictly "natural." This isn't surprising either, since what we call "nature" is a "denatured," unnatural, uncanny sequence of mutations and catastrophic events: just read Darwin. The ecological view to come isn't a picture of some bounded object or "restrictive economy," a closed system.[19] It is a vast, sprawling mesh of interconnection without a definite center or edge. It is radical intimacy, coexistence with other beings, sentient and otherwise—and how can we so clearly tell the difference? The ecological thought fans out into questions concerning cyborgs, artificial intelligence, and the irreducible uncertainty over what counts as a person.[20] Being a person means never being sure that you're one. In an age of ecology without Nature, we would treat many more beings as people while deconstructing our ideas about what counts as people. Think *Blade Runner* or *Frankenstein:* the ethics of the ecological thought is to regard beings as people even when they aren't people. Ancient animisms treat beings as people, without a concept of Nature. Perhaps I'm aiming for an upgraded version of animism. (I'm also aiming for another good excuse to write about my favorite film, *Blade Runner.*)

OPENING MOVES

Thinking the ecological thought is difficult: it involves becoming open, radically open—open forever, without the possibility of closing again. Studying art provides a platform, because the environment is partly a matter of perception. Art forms have something to tell us about the environment, because they can make us question reality. I would like to stay for as long as possible in an open, questioning mode. This open mode is intrinsic to whatever we inadequately call the environment.[21] Is the ecological thought thinking about ecology? Yes and no. It is a thinking that is ecological, a contemplating that is a doing. Reframing our world, our problems, and ourselves is part of the ecological project. This is what *praxis* means—action that is thoughtful and thought that is active. Aristotle asserted that the highest form of praxis was contemplation.[22] We shouldn't be afraid to withdraw and reflect.

The ecological thought is also difficult because it brings to light aspects of our existence that have remained unconscious for a long time; we don't like to recall them. It isn't *like* thinking about where your toilet waste goes. It *is* thinking about where your toilet waste goes. Anxiety over wastewater treatment provides a good example. In the United States, many people now drink recycled wastewater. Some people simply don't want to know that their water is recycled excrement. It is public policy to tune out this fact. Yet recycled water is less unclean than "naturally" filtered water. We lose not only our undisturbed dreams of civilized cleanliness through this process but also our sense of Nature as pristine and nonartificial. Nature becomes wastewater treatment version 1.0.[23] Freud described the unconscious as a wilderness area. Wilderness areas are the unconscious of modern society, places we can go to keep our dreams undisturbed. The very form of modern consciousness is itself this dream.

In Lakewood, Colorado, residents objected to the construction of a solar array in a park in 2008, because it didn't look "natural."[24] Objections to wind farms are similar—made not because of the risk to birds but because they "spoil the view." A 2008 plan to put a wind farm near a remote Scottish island was, well, scotched, because residents complained that their view would be destroyed. This is truly a case of the aesthetics of Nature impeding ecology and a good argument for why ecology must be without Nature. Why is a wind turbine less beautiful than an oil pipe? Why does it "spoil the view" any more than pipes and roads?

You could see turbines as environmental art. Wind chimes play in the wind; some environmental sculptures sway and rock in the breeze. Wind farms have a slightly frightening size and magnificence. One could easily read them as embodying the aesthetics of the sublime (rather than the beautiful). But it's an ethical sublime that says, "We humans choose not to use carbon"—a choice visible in gigantic turbines. Perhaps it's this very visibility of choice that makes wind farms disturbing: visible choice, rather than secret pipes, running under an apparently undisturbed "landscape" (a word for a painting, not actual trees and water). As a poster in the office of Mulder in the television series *The X-Files* used to read, "The Truth Is Out There." Ideology isn't just in your head. It's in the shape of a Coke bottle. It's in the way some things appear "natural"—rolling hills and greenery—as if the Industrial Revolution had never occurred. These fake landscapes are the original greenwashing. What the Scots are saying, in objecting to wind farms, isn't "Save the environment!" but "Leave our dreams undisturbed!"

If you're a parent, you will understand our resistance to cleaning things up. Ecology talks about areas of life that we find annoying, boring, and embarrassing. Art can help us, because it's a place in our culture that deals with intensity, shame, abjection, and loss. It also deals with reality and un-reality, being and seeming. If ecology is about radical coexistence, then we must challenge our sense of what is real and what is unreal, what counts as existent and what counts as nonexistent. The idea of Nature as a holistic, healthy, real thing avoids this challenge.

We must face some puzzling questions. What is an environment? Is there such a thing as *the environment?* Is it everything "around" us? At what point do we stop, if at all, drawing the line between *environment* and *non-environment:* The atmosphere? Earth's gravitational field? Earth's magnetic field, without which everything would be scorched by solar winds? The sun, without which we wouldn't be alive at all? The Galaxy? Does the en-vironment include or exclude us? Is it natural or artificial, or both? Can we put it in a conceptual box? Might the word *environment* be the wrong word? *Environment*, the upgrade of *Nature*, is fraught with difficulty. This is ironic, since what we often call the environment is being changed, degraded, and eroded (and destroyed) by global forces of industry and capitalism. Just when we need to know what it is, it's disappearing.

Along with the ecological crisis goes an equally powerful and urgent opening up of our view of who we are and where we are. What, therefore, is environmental art? If what we inadequately call the environment entails a radical openness, how does this appear in art forms? Are there environ-mental ways of reading and doing criticism that account for this radical openness? Various kinds of ecocriticism have emerged to explore the role of ecology in literature. In particular, Romantic literature, from the be-ginning of the modern age of industry and capitalism, has served as a touchstone for ecocriticism.[25] This brand of criticism, however, restricts the radical openness the ecological thought implies, employing a pre-packaged conceptual container labeled "Nature." Ironically, Romantic "Nature" is an artificial construct. And extra-ironically, Romantic-period art itself already thought about the environment in ways that were decisively "out of the box." We will thus find it helpful to explore Romantic literature in *The Ecological Thought*.[26] Nothing much has changed since. There is more concrete, more plastic, more democracy, more intense science and technology, more GDP, more alienation, and more self-consciousness about whether writing poems really can change the world. These are quantitative differences, not qualitative ones.

A truly ecological reading practice would think the environment beyond rigid conceptual categories—it would include as much as possible of the radical openness of the ecological thought. Ecocriticism has overlooked the way in which all art—not just explicitly ecological art—hardwires the environment into its *form*. Ecological art, and the ecological-ness of all art, isn't just *about* something (trees, mountains, animals, pollution, and so forth). Ecological art *is* something, or maybe it *does* something. Art is ecological insofar as it is made from materials and exists in the world. It exists, for instance, as a poem on a page made of paper from trees, which you hold in your hand while sitting in a chair in a certain room of a house that rests on a hill in the suburbs of a polluted city. But there is more to its ecological quality than that. The shape of the stanzas and the length of the lines determine the way you appreciate the blank paper around them. Reading the poem aloud makes you aware of the shape and size of the space around you (some forms, such as yodeling, do this deliberately). The poem organizes space. Seen like this, all texts—all artworks, indeed—have an irreducibly ecological form. Ecology permeates all forms. Nowadays we're used to wondering what a poem says about race or gender, even if the poem makes no explicit mention of race or gender. We will soon be accustomed to wondering what any text says about the environment even if no animals or trees or mountains appear in it.[27]

The ecological thought affects all aspects of life, culture, and society. Aside from art and science, we must build the ecological thought from what we find in philosophy, history, sociology, anthropology, religion, cultural studies, and critical theory. I shall combine empirical evolution

theory with "Continental" thinking about being and existence. This seems
perverse: "high" philosophy merging shamelessly with "vulgar" materialism. There are pretty good boundaries between science and humanities
departments and within the humanities themselves. This won't be to everyone's taste. Daniel Dennett, a Darwinist cognition theorist, pooh-poohs
deconstruction.[28] Much Continental thinking assumes that there is no
continuity between humans and animals, adopting a haughty "everyone
knows that" tone and declaring that thinking otherwise is "asinine" (worse
than asinine—and worse because we're behaving like donkeys).[29] This is
condescending exclusivity. Some insist proudly that they "refuse to accept
the theory of evolution," which to a biologist sounds like refusing to
accept that the Earth is round.[30] Even creationists take evolution more
seriously than that. It doesn't have to be like this. No less a figure than
Derrida maintained that deconstruction was a form of radical empiricism.[31]
You want anti-essentialism and antibiologism? Just read Darwin.

Taken at their trivial and ideological worst, the humanities is hamstrung by "factoids," quasi- or pseudofacts that haven't been well thought
out, while the sciences are held in the sway of unconscious "opinions."
Humanities and sciences hold broken pieces of a jigsaw puzzle, pieces that
might not fit together. Like William Blake I'm suspicious of "fitting &
fitted."[32] The ecological thought must interrogate both the attitude of
science, its detached authoritarian coldness; and the nihilistic, baselessly
anthropocentric arguments in the humanities as well as humanist refusals
to see the big picture, often justified by self-limiting arguments against
"totalization"—talk about shooting yourself in the foot.[33] The ecological
thought is about warmth and strangeness, infinity and proximity, tantalizing "thereness" and head-popping, wordless openness.

The ecological thought is intrinsically open, so it doesn't really matter
where you begin. There are good reasons for trusting the biases and spe-
cialties that I bring to this task. Studying art is important, because art sometimes gives voice to what is unspeakable elsewhere, either temporarily—
one day we will find the words—or intrinsically—words are impossible.
Since the ecological thought is so new and so open, and therefore so difficult, we should expect art to show us some of the way. The ecological
thought supplies good reasons to study culture and philosophy. Ecology is
a matter of human experience. Humanities research can ask questions

that science should address, questions that scientists may not have asked yet. For its part, science is about being able to admit that you're wrong. This means that if we want to live in a science-based society, we will have to live in the shadow of the possibility of wrongness. A questioning attitude needs to become habitual. Philosophy and critical theory in the humanities can help. Some people, including left humanities scholars who should know better, either think that scientists should be left to get on with their work, or even when they don't, the net effect of their beliefs is that science is untouched.[34] We have a responsibility to examine, participate in, support, and criticize scientific experiments: to that end, this book shall propose some.

For example, are nonhumans capable of aesthetic contemplation? Can they enjoy art? Fascinating research projects, to say the least, are beginning find out whether the beings we call animals are capable of this. If they were, it would be essential to find out whether this contemplation was an advanced cognitive state or a simple one, if not the simplest. Is our capacity to enjoy art one of those things that makes us uniquely human (along with hands, tools, laughter, and dancing, all of which have been discovered in nonhumans)? Or do we share this capacity with nonhuman beings? These questions get to the heart of some of our cultural and political assumptions regarding nonhuman beings.

While it's deeply informed by critical theory, this book won't be talking very explicitly about theory. Why? Not because I want to dumb down the argument. I do this because people who aren't members of the in crowd of specialists familiar with the language of theory (and the kinds of things that are cool to say with it) badly need to read this book. Otherwise the ecological thought separates theory haves from have-nots. Humanities scholars have some very good and important ideas, if only they would let others read them. We simply can't leave environmentalism to the anti-intellectualists. If you're interested, this book does engage with theory in the notes. Or you can read my essays, perhaps starting with "Queer Ecology" in *PMLA*, and also *Ecology without Nature*.[35] I won't be doing a lot of green close reading either. You can find some examples, based on the view this book lays out, by following this note.[36]

THE CHAPTERS IN THIS BOOK

Current ecological scholarship in the humanities is divided between ecocriticism, environmental justice criticism, science studies ethnography and anthropological investigations of non-Western environmental perception; and there is a growing body of philosophical and theoretically oriented work. The humanities are where we reflect on culture, politics, and science. If they mean anything at all in this age of scientism, the humanities must do serious reflection. While we address the current ecological crisis, we should regard this moment as a precious, if perilous, opportunity to think some difficult thoughts about what ecology is.

Ecological science has to model ecosystems on different scales in order to see things properly: it's not enough to section off a small square of reality and just examine that.[37] This is very suggestive for aesthetic and political thinking. Chapter 1, "Thinking Big," argues that for the ecological thought to lift off, it must escape some terms in which it has been trapped. Terms such as the local, the organic, and the particular have been good for environmentalist social policy. These ideas provide at least a pocket of resistance to globalization. But what about global warming? Doesn't that make a global response necessary? How about the fact that we're witnessing the Sixth Mass Extinction Event? Ecological thinking risks being caught in the language of smallness and restriction. I use Milton to kick off the discussion, because he offers us one of the most immense viewpoints of all: that of space itself. Seeing the Earth from space is the beginning of ecological thinking. The first aeronauts, balloon pilots, immediately saw Earth as an alien world.[38] Seeing yourself from another point of view is the beginning of ethics and politics.

Chapter 1 introduces two ideas within the ecological thought—the *mesh* and the *strange stranger*. When we think big, curious things happen. People commonly criticize science for disenchanting the world, making it both utterly flat and highly profitable, to parody Hamlet. Science isn't necessarily enchanting, but I shall suggest that the more we know, the less certain and the more ambiguous things become, both on a micro and on a macro level. The current ecological disaster, which we know about only because of very sophisticated interdisciplinary science, has torn a giant hole in the fabric of our understanding. This isn't just because the world has already changed utterly. It is also because of the philosophical and experiential implications of the crisis that engendered the ecological thought. The ecological thought imagines interconnectedness, which I call *the mesh*. Who or what is interconnected with what or with whom? The mesh of interconnected things is vast, perhaps immeasurably so. Each entity in the mesh looks strange. Nothing exists all by itself, and so nothing is fully "itself." There is curiously "less" of the Universe at the same time, and for the same reasons, as we see "more" of it. Our encounter with other beings becomes profound. They are strange, even intrinsically strange. Getting to know them makes them stranger. When we talk about life forms, we're talking about *strange strangers*.[39] The ecological thought imagines a multitude of entangled strange strangers.

How do we get inspired to think as big as the ecological thought requires? In Chapter 1, I explore some literary, artistic, and cultural forms that can help us. There is, for example, a counterstrain in literary "green" writing that has not so much to do with hedgerows and birds' nests as it has to do with the planet Earth as a whole and with the displacement and disorientation we feel when we start to think big. Milton is the forerunner here, but Wordsworth also shows up, along with the very Wordsworth people associate with green Wellington boots, muddy Volvos, and quaint nooks of mythical Olde England. When we think of indigenous cultures, we tend to impose a Western ideology of localism and "small is beautiful" onto them. In the case of at least one culture—nomadic Tibetans—this is a big mistake. Should we wish to send astronauts to Mars, we could do worse than train Tibetans and other indigenous peoples for the ride. They would only have to learn to push a few buttons. The very people we think of as thinking small may think the biggest of all.

The ecological thought is as much about opening our minds as it is about *knowing* something or other in particular. At its limit, it is a radical openness to everything. The ecological thought is therefore full of shadows and twilights. The ecological world isn't a positive, sunny "Zippity Doo Da" world.[40] The sentimental aesthetics of cute animals is obviously an obstacle to the ecological thought. But so is the sublime aesthetics of the awesome. We need a whole new way of evoking the environment. In this respect, utopian eco-language turns me off. It is far too affirmative. This is one reason why Chapter 2 is called "Dark Thoughts." I am perhaps unfairly nauseated by the idea of "bright green"—a shade of environmental think-ing that recently gained some popularity.⁴¹ "Bright" conveys optimism, intelligence, and an acceptance of the sunny world of consumer products. The inventors claim that ecological thinking can accommodate itself to postmodern consumer capitalism. Maybe at heart I'm an old-fashioned goth, but when I hear the word "bright" I reach for my sunglasses. The ecological thought is intrinsically dark, mysterious, and open, like an empty city square at dusk, a half-open door, or an unresolved chord. It is realis-tic, depressing, intimate, and alive and ironic all at the same time. It is no wonder that the ancients thought that melancholy, their word for depres-sion, was the earth mood. In the language of humor theory, melancholy is black, earthy, and cold.

Environmental rhetoric is too often strongly affirmative, extraverted, and masculine; it privileges speech over writing; and it simulates imme-diacy (feigning one-to-one correspondences between language and real-ity). It's sunny, straightforward, ableist, holistic, hearty, and "healthy." Where does this leave negativity, introversion, femininity, writing, me-diation, ambiguity, darkness, irony, fragmentation, and sickness? Are these simply nonecological categories? Must we accept the injunction to turn on, tune in, shut up, go outdoors, and breathe Nature? Are we ostriches compelled to stick our ironic heads in the sand for fear of embarrassing Nature? I don't think so. If the ecological thought is as big as I think it is, it must include darkness as well as light, negativity as well as positivity.

Negativity might even be more ecological than positivity is. A truly scientific attitude means not believing everything you think. This means that your thinking keeps encountering nonidentical phenomena, things you can't put in a box. If the ecological thought is scientific, this implies that it has a high tolerance for negativity. Psychoanalysis asserts that melan-cholia bonds us inextricably to the mother's body. Are we similarly bonded to Earth itself? Is the dark experience of separateness from Earth a place where we can experience ecological awareness? Is loneliness a sign of deep connection? Chapter 2 answers "yes" to these questions.

I explore the possibility of a new ecological aesthetics: *dark ecology*. Dark ecology puts hesitation, uncertainty, irony, and thoughtfulness back into ecological thinking. The form of dark ecology is that of noir film. The noir narrator begins investigating a supposedly external situation, from a supposedly neutral point of view, only to discover that she or he is implicated in it. The point of view of the narrator herself becomes stained with desire. There is no metaposition from which we can make ecological pronouncements. Ironically, this applies in particular to the sunny, affirmative rhetoric of environmental ideology. A more honest ecological art would linger in the shadowy world of irony and difference. With dark ecology, we can explore all kinds of art forms as ecological: not just ones that are about lions and mountains, not just journal writing and sublimity. The ecological thought includes negativity and irony, ugliness and horror. Democracy is well served by irony, because irony insists that there are other points of view that we must acknowledge. Ugliness and horror are important, because they compel our compassionate coexistence to go beyond condescending pity.

Things will get worse before they get better, if at all. We must create frameworks for coping with a catastrophe that, from the evidence of the hysterical announcements of its imminent arrival, *has already occurred.*

Chapter 2 provides extra shading to the idea of strange strangers, the life forms to whom we find ourselves connected. The strange stranger is at the limit of our imagining. As well as being about melancholy, dark ecology is also about uncertainty. Even if biology knew all the species on Earth, we would still encounter them as strange strangers, because of the inner logic of knowledge. The more you know about something, the stranger it grows. The more you know about the origins of the First World War, the more ambiguous your conclusions become. You find yourself unable to point to a single independent event. Viewed from a distance, the United Kingdom looks like a triangle. When you view it at a scale of millimeters, it looks very crinkly.[42] The more we know about life forms, the more we recognize our connection with them and the stranger they become. The strange stranger isn't just a blank at the end of a long list of life forms we know (aardvarks, beetles, chameleons . . . the strange stranger). The strange stranger lives within (and without) each and every being. Along the way toward this idea, we visit the philosophy of consciousness, and in particular theories of artificial intelligence. Animals and robots (and computers) are often held in the same (low) esteem.

The more you know, the more entangled you realize you are, and the more open and ambiguous everything becomes. Consider the final paragraph of *The Origin of Species:*

It is interesting to contemplate an entangled bank, clothed with many plants of many kinds, with birds singing on the bushes, with various insects flitting about, and with worms crawling through the damp earth, and to reflect that these elaborately constructed forms, so different from each other, and dependent on each other in so complex a manner, have all been produced by laws acting around us. These laws, taken in the largest sense, being Growth with Reproduction; Inheritance . . . ; Variability, from the indirect and direct action of the conditions of life, and from use and disuse; a Ratio of Increase so high as to lead to a Struggle for Life, and as a consequent to Natural Selection, entailing Divergence of Character and the Extinction of less-improved forms.[43]

Throughout this book, I return to Darwin, because it is Darwin who thought through many of the complex and hard-to-face issues that confront the ecological thought. Modern thinking is willfully ignorant of Darwin. What does it feel like to understand evolution? Are we ready to admit the world of mutation and uncertainty that Darwin opens up?

Evolutionary biology must take art into account. The theory of sexual selection suggests that life manifests profound elements of sheer display, as any self-respecting mandrill or bowerbird could tell you. There are no realms more ambiguous than those of language and art. Camouflage, deception, and pure appearance are the stock in trade of life forms. Language provides evidence of the reduplication and random mutation that make up the processes of evolution. The strange stranger is involved in a shifting zone of aesthetic seeming and illusion. A rigorous thinking of the ecological thought compels us to let go of the unitary, virile ideas of Nature and the Natural that still prevail. The ecological thought is intrinsically queer. (Joining ecological thinking with thinking on gender and sexuality would make a fantastic bang, and this alone is reason enough to try it.) Finally, Chapter 2 shows that even at the furthest reaches of supposedly anti-ecological thinking, we find traces of the ecological thought. This is good news: it means that everything is ultimately workable and that the ecological thought, while hard to think thoroughly, is easy to latch onto from anywhere.

The ecological thought thinks big and joins the dots. It thinks through the mesh of life forms as far out and in as it can. It comes as close as possible to the strange stranger, generating care and concern for beings, no matter how uncertain we are of their identity, no matter how afraid we are of their existence. How do we proceed? Chapter 3, "Forward Thinking," argues that these are not the end times but the first glimmerings of new times. The ecological thought must transcend the language of apocalypse. It's ironic that we can imagine the collapse of the Antarctic ice shelves more readily than we can the collapse of the banking system—and despite this, amazingly, as this book was written, the banking system did collapse. The ecological thought must imagine economic change; otherwise it's just another piece on the game board of capitalist ideology. The boring, rapacious reality we have constructed, with its familiar, furious, yet ultimately static whirl, isn't the final state of history. The ecological society to come will be much more pleasurable, far more sociable, and ever so much more reasonable than we can imagine.

Ecology equals living minus Nature, plus consciousness. There are some tentative, shadowy models in art to show us the way. I explore how they direct us toward an ecological view. These models include experiments in artistic form as well as special kinds of artistic content. Chapter 3 explores progressive ideas in philosophy, science, economics, politics, and religion. It also examines one of the longest-term ecological problems: how to deal with the existence of *hyperobjects*, products such as Styrofoam and plutonium that exist on almost unthinkable timescales. Like the strange stranger, these materials confound our limited, fixated, self-oriented frameworks.

Our current categories are not set in stone. Capitalism isn't the Procrustean bed that stretches everything to fit it forever. In the future, people might see what we now call postmodern art and culture as the emergence of global environmental culture. Like a virus, the ecological thought infects other systems of thinking and alters them from within, gradually disabling the incompatible ones. The infection has only just begun.

1
Thinking Big

The whole of the gene pool of the biosphere is available to all organisms.

Kwang W. Jeon and James F. Danielli

Small is beautiful. Diet for a small planet. The local is better than the global. These are some of the slogans of environmental movements since the late 1960s.[1] I'll be proposing the exact opposite of the sentiments they express. In my formulation, the best environmental thinking is thinking big—as big as possible, and maybe even bigger than that, bigger than we can conceive. The philosopher Immanuel Kant said that the sublime could be the idea of bigness beyond any ability to measure or picture—magnitude beyond any idea of magnitude. In its profundity and vastness, this magnitude demonstrates the radical freedom of our minds to transcend our "reality," the given state of affairs. Like operating system software, it doesn't tell us what to think, but it boots up our minds to be ready for what we need in thinking democracy.[2] And it's also what we need in thinking ecology.

Witness this new-made world, another Heav'n
From Heaven gate not far, founded in view

On the clear hyaline, the glassy sea;
Of amplitude almost immense, with stars
Numerous, and every star perhaps a world
Of destined habitation; but thou know'st
Their seasons: among these the seat of men,
Earth with her nether Ocean circumfused,
Their pleasant dwelling place.

(John Milton, *Paradise Lost* 7.617–625)

What if that light
Sent from her through the wide transpicuous air,
To the terrestrial moon be as a star
Enlight'ning her by day, as she by night
This earth? reciprocal, if land be there,
Fields and inhabitants: her spots thou seest
As clouds, and clouds may rain, and rain produce
Fruits in her softened soil, for some to eat
Allotted there; and other suns perhaps
With their attendant moons, thou wilt descry
Communicating male and female light,
Which two great sexes animate the world,
Stored in each orb perhaps with some that live.
For such vast room in Nature unpossessed
By living soul, desért and desolate,
Only to shine, yet scarce to cóntribute
Each orb a glimpse of light, conveyed so far
Down to this habitable, which returns
Light back to them, is obvious to dispute.

(8.140–158)[3]

There's a decisive moment in the angel Raphael's conversation with Adam in John Milton's epic poem *Paradise Lost*. Raphael is warning Adam against the dangers of speculation. Idle flights of fancy could divert one from just and temperate action. But Raphael uses the form of a negative injunction, like the modern-day equivalent, "Don't think of a pink elephant!" Too late: we, and Adam, have already thought of it. What is the pink elephant?

It's an image of other possible Edens on other planets, other atmospheres, other ecosystems "with . . . Ocean circumfused" (7.624). Raphael points to the stars and the Moon. Who knows, he says, perhaps there are extraterrestrial Gardens of Eden up there, on which an alien Adam and another Raphael are conversing. Raphael reinforces this in book 8, suggesting that there may be livable worlds beyond Earth.

What an extraordinary moment in the history of the ecological thought! Instead of saying, "You are here. Get used to it," Raphael offers a negative image of human location, suggesting that humans shouldn't think that their planet is the only important one. The angel's language makes good theological sense. If they refrain from thinking that they are too important, humans will resist Satan's setting up of humans at the center of a Universe that, like the apple, is there for the taking. Eden is surrounded by other worlds. The stars are not just a light show (8.153). It's not only a vast Universe that Raphael is revealing but also an intimate one—the stars are peopled.[4] This is an amazing affront to the idea of the uniqueness of "mankind," and Raphael prohibits it even as he permits it.

According to this Universe's eye view, humans must not act from a sense of irrational spontaneous connectedness. Instead, Raphael suggests, they must reflect rationally on their decentered place in the Universe— and on their inability to account for this disorientation. Raphael's injunction liberates reason and speculative enjoyment (what kinds of fruit do they eat up there?). It opens the capacity for fantasy while restraining it, such that the promise of complete knowledge always exceeds its conditions. And yet this very excess (of accurate thought) is what the injunction permits.

We can't see everywhere. We can't see everywhere all at once (not even with Google Earth). When we look at x, we can't look at y. Cognitive science suggests that our perception is quantized—it comes in little packets, not a continuous flow.[5] Our perception is full of holes. The nothingness in perception—we can't plumb the depths of space—is the basis for Raphael's injunction not to think of other planets. The infinite is not an object to be seen.[6]

Raphael doesn't claim that extraterrestrials exist: that's the whole point. The mere possibility of extraterrestrial environments and sentient beings—their possibility (hypothetical but imperceptible) is their essence— provides the fantasy point from which the reader herself, like Adam and

Eve, can achieve the "impossible" viewpoint of space. To reach this stand-point involves an act of rational self-reflection independent of graven im-ages. This "impossible" viewpoint is a cornerstone of the ecological thought.

Raphael is saying, "There may be things beyond your ken, but that is beyond your ken." The statement pulls the rug out from under its own feet. Under the rug is a sky filled with stars, and there might be other minds out there. That subjunctive *might be* is important. Milton deals with the hypothetical, because having a hypothesis means having an open mind—perhaps the supposition is wrong. Raphael is hesitant, not authori-tative. The iconoclastic Milton studiously avoids the touchy-feely, ulti-mately authoritarian organicism upon which claims of interconnected-ness are usually built—organicism being an aesthetic image of a "natural" fit between form and content and between parts and the whole. While Adam and Eve inhabit the Garden of Eden, they aren't shut off from the rest of the Universe. Humans must act not because a powerful authority figure has told them to but via a sense of the openness of space. It's a different way of imagining what ecology means, without the coziness of Noah's ark. According to this view, we care for what surrounds us not because God commanded us to, nor because of some authoritarian "truthi-ness," but because of reason.

Milton achieves the ecological thought in form as well as in content. The versification opens wide, freed from what he called "the modern bond-age of rhyming."[7] The very air that Raphael describes is "transpicuous" (8.141). Earth's atmosphere is pellucid and transparent, allowing the pas-sage of light and hence knowledge. Earth and the distant stars and planets send light to each other (156–158). This dynamic reciprocity of light is like a republic, even a democracy. Scanning the words on the page, the reader must perform this herself. Our eyes have to "return" as we venture out into the space on the right of the page, then voyage back to the next line. We're placed in the position of one of the far-off worlds, gazing back at Earth. We have been teleported. We see ourselves from the point of view of outer space. Milton loves this point of view. He uses it elsewhere in *Paradise Lost* to make Satan look really small—we see him as if through the wrong end of a telescope (3.590). Satan stands for the puffed-up ego that wants to be seen as really big. The title of this chapter, "Thinking Big," is supposed to make us feel humble, not proud.

Like Milton, we live in an age of astronomy. "Earthrise," the image of Earth from space taken by the Apollo 11 mission, is now an icon. Milton would have liked it. He would probably not have considered it an icon but as iconoclastic. He would have enjoyed how it displaces our sense of centrality, making us see ourselves from the outside. Percy Shelley used the image in his radical poem *Queen Mab*. The fairy Mab takes a little girl up into outer space to see Earth from a distance and to contemplate the miseries of human history:

> Earth's distant orb appeared
> The smallest light that twinkles in the heaven;
> Whilst round the chariot's way
> Innumerable systems rolled
> And countless spheres diffused
> An ever-varying glory.   (1.250–255)[8]

Distance doesn't mean indifference, and coolness (using reason) isn't coldness. Environmental language frequently urges us to get hot under the collar. The ecological thought aims for something cooler, at least at first. Al Gore and others have used "Earthrise" to induce us to hold and care for Earth, as if it were a fragile ball of glass. *Universe*, a magnificent animated film from Canada (1960), and the opening sequence of the film *Contact*, based on Carl Sagan's novel, travel out, and out, and out, from Earth into the Universe.[9] They are zooms from nowhere. Archimedes said, "Give me somewhere to stand, and I shall move the Earth." The ecological thought says, "Give us nowhere to stand, and we shall care for the Earth."

We no longer live within a horizon (did we ever?). We no longer live in a place where the sun comes up and goes down, no matter how much some philosophers insist that we experience things that way. We've lost a sense of the significance of events that appear on horizons (did we ever have them?). Strange configurations of stars or lights and clouds in the sky, like some cosmic being's writing, have disappeared. (An old joke: "Red sky at night, shepherd's house on fire; red sky in the morning— shepherd's house still on fire.") Space isn't something that happens beyond the ionosphere. We are in space right now.

We can appreciate the fragility of our world from the point of view of space. Thinking big doesn't prevent us from caring for the environment.[10]

Google Earth and Google Maps make this vision a matter of pointing and clicking. Some object that these technologies are mass surveillance. They would be right. Only in an age of this "power-knowledge" can global awareness become available for Western rationalists. Google Earth enabled us to see that cows align north to south across the planet.[11] This knowledge was unavailable to people supposedly "embedded" in a "lifeworld." Consider how we're now aware of risks on global and micro scales. We can find out exactly how much mercury our bodies contain. We know that popular kinds of plastic leach dioxins. The more risk we know about, the more risk spreads. Risk becomes democratized, and democracy becomes about managing risk. Ulrich Beck calls it a "risk society": how our increasing awareness of risk in all dimensions (across space, within our bodies, over time) changes our awareness of how we coexist.[12] We can't "unthink" risk. Along with the sense of tremendous power and voyeuristic, sadistic fantasies of being able to see everything (on Google Earth, YouTube, and so on) goes a sense of perilous vulnerability.

TIBETANS IN SPACE

Do we have to go into outer space to care for Earth? Do we need high technology? Do we need Google Earth to imagine Earth? Is Western science and power the only path to ecological awareness? Many environmentalists would throw up their hands at my assumptions here. First of all, isn't Western society and all it stands for (the dreaded Cartesian dualism, "technology" and its by-products) precisely what we must destroy or retreat from? And don't so-called prehistoric, pretechnological societies hold keys to our salvation?

No. Consider a society that has developed the ecological thought outside the scope of Western culture: Tibet. Old Tibet hardly even had wheels, except prayer wheels. Yet Tibetans had ideas of big space and big time when in the West these would have been heresy.

There is a lot to say about modern Tibet, perhaps too much—an endless succession of checkpoints; prisoners digging roads with their bare hands; the way Tibetans are treated like Native Americans were during the pioneering days; New Age appropriations of their culture, as if the nineteenth and twenty-first centuries were happening simultaneously. I will avoid that and head straight for an insight. It's the "West" that fixates on place, thinking that there's this thing called "place" that is solid and real and independent and that has been progressively undermined by modernity, capitalism, technology, you name it. Fixation on place impedes a truly ecological view.

Before I went to Tibet, I wondered whether indigenous people actually did have an "authentic," "non-Western" experience of place. I returned less sure than ever. When you camp in Tibet, as I did for about two weeks, you sleep under outer space—as directly below it as you can get without flying. The Tibetan plateau is about 16,500 feet above sea level on average: you can pretty much walk to the second base camp of Everest from the town of Tingri (a twenty-one-mile hike across a flat plain). Look up at a plane: at four times higher than that, you're not even close.

The surface of the Tibetan plateau is already like the surface of Mars. Above me, the Milky Way never looked so big. Imagine a really wide carpet runner. Now multiply that by about three. Fill it with thousands of points of dustlike stars. Add about thirty new stars to the Big Dipper. Imagine shooting stars so frequent you don't have to look for more than half an hour to see about ten. Some of them make a sound as they burn up in the atmosphere. One shooting star was about the diameter of half a one-cent coin and fizzed as it swept across the sky like ice cream in Coca-Cola.

Tibetans live very close to outer space, so it's not surprising that they include it in their culture. When asked where he came from, the first Bön king (Bön is the indigenous culture) pointed up to the sky. No, I'm not saying that Tibetans came from outer space. The tantric teachings say there are 6,400,000 Tantras of Dzogchen (texts of a form of Tibetan Buddhism). On Earth we have seventeen. Up there, in the highly visible night sky, perhaps in other universes, there exist the remaining 6,399,983. Up there, someone is meditating.

Tibetans would make the best space pilots, especially for long space missions. They would need to learn only how to operate the equipment. Tibetan culture and religion is all about space. All kinds of images entice us to think big. One image of enlightened mind is that it's like space. One Buddhist system says that our Universe, along with one billion universes like it, floats within a single pollen grain inside an anther on a lotus flower growing out of a begging bowl in the hands of a Buddha called Immense

Ocean Vairochana.[13] Tibetans would arrive at the edge of the Solar System and declare, "Wow, what a great opportunity to learn more about emptiness." Outer space wouldn't undermine their "beliefs."

Does this sound like primitivism? Primitivists maintain there was a time—call it a golden age, call it "prehistory"—when human beings didn't do all the bad things they do today, when they had better social systems, enjoyed more pleasures, and so on. Some primitivists believe that holdout societies persist somewhere on Earth. I would have accused anyone talking like this of just such a fantasy before I went to Tibet. Tibetans have a great appreciation for inner space. So they would thrive in outer space. Tibetans do not belong in the past or in a museum. They belong in the future.

Thinking big doesn't contradict concern for minute particulars. Christian apocalypticism shares with deep ecology a fundamental lack of concern for the way things are going. Since the end of the world is nigh, or since we will all become extinct in the long run, there isn't much point in caring. Their view of outer space doesn't prevent the Tibetans from having developed ideas about compassion and nonviolence and a remarkable system of restorative justice.[14]

In the West, we think of ecology as earthbound. Not only earthbound: we want ecology to be about location, location, location. In particular, location must be local: it must feel like home; we must recognize it and think it in terms of the here and now, not the there and then. For the philosopher Martin Heidegger, thinking itself was an environmental presence, as the word "dwelling" suggests. When we dwell on something, we inhabit it. Originally, for Heidegger, thinking dwelt upon the Earth.[15] It is ironic that Heidegger thought he was thinking like a peasant. No self-respecting Tibetan peasant would think like that. She would be much more likely to say, like the rock band Spiritualized, "Ladies and gentlemen, we are floating in space."[16] The localism meme will compel westerners to eat each other as soon as they get beyond the Asteroid Belt.

Heidegger's environmentalism is a sad, fascist, stunted bonsai version, forced to grow in a tiny iron flowerpot by a cottage in the German Black Forest. We can do better. Rather than cowering or running away, we can beat Heidegger at his own game. You want religious language? Look up at the Milky Way. Imagine n-thousand habitable worlds, filled with sentient beings wondering just how vast the ecological thought is. Could we have a progressive ecology that was big, not small; spacious, not place-ist; global, not local (if not universal); not embodied but displaced, spaced, outer spaced? Our slogan should be dislocation, dislocation, dislocation.

THE MESH: A TRULY WONDERFUL FACT

We can no longer have that reassuringly trivial conversation about the weather with someone in the street, as a way to break the ice or pass the time. The conversation either trails off into a disturbingly meaningful silence, or someone mentions global warming. The weather no longer exists as a neutral-seeming background against which events take place. When weather becomes climate—when it enters the realms of science and history—it can no longer be a stage set. You can't visualize the climate. Mapping it requires a processing speed in terabytes per second (a terabyte is a thousand gigabytes).[17]

The weather withers because of our increasing awareness of the *mesh*. Most words I considered to describe interdependence were compromised by references to the Internet—like "network." Either that, or they were compromised by vitalism, the belief in a living substance. "Web" is a little bit too vitalist and a little bit Internet-ish for my taste, so it loses on both counts. "Mesh" is short, shorter in particular than "the interconnectedness of all living and non-living things."

"Mesh" can mean the holes in a network and threading between them. It suggests both hardness and delicacy. It has uses in biology, mathematics, and engineering and in weaving and computing—think stockings and graphic design, metals and fabrics. It has antecedents in *mask* and *mass*, suggesting both density and deception.[18] By extension, "mesh" can mean "a complex situation or series of events in which a person is entangled; a concatenation of constraining or restricting forces or circumstances; a snare."[19] In other words, it's perfect.

The ecological thought stirs because the mesh appears in our social, psychic, and scientific domains. Since everything is interconnected, there is no definite background and therefore no definite foreground. Darwin sensed the mesh while pondering the implications of natural selection. You can detect Darwin's amazement:

It is a truly wonderful fact—the wonder of which we are apt to over-look through familiarity—that all animals and all plants throughout all time and space should be related to each other in group subordinate to group . . . varieties of the same species most closely related to-gether, species of the same genus less closely and unequally related together, forming sections and sub-genera, species of distinct genera much less closely related, and genera related in different degrees, forming sub-families, families, orders, sub-classes, and classes. The several subordinate groups in any class cannot be ranked in a single file, but seem rather to be clustered round points, and these round in other points, and so on in almost endless cycles.[20]

Every single life form is literally familiar: we're genetically descended from them. Darwin imagines an endlessly branching tree. In contrast, *mesh* doesn't suggest a clear starting point, and those "clusters" of "subordinate groups" are far from linear (they "cannot be ranked in a single file"). Each point of the mesh is both the center and edge of a system of points, so there is no absolute center or edge. Still, the tree image provides a marvelous way of ending the chapter on natural selection: "the Great Tree of Life, which fills with its dead and broken branches the crust of the Earth, and covers the surface with its ever branching and beautiful ramifications."[21] A "rami-fication" is a branch and an implication, a branching thought. Darwin brings ecological interconnectedness and thinking together.

The ecological thought does, indeed, consist in the ramifications of the "truly wonderful fact" of the mesh. All life forms are the mesh, and so are all dead ones, as are their habitats, which are also made up of living and nonliving beings. We know even more now about how life forms have shaped Earth (think of oil, of oxygen—the first climate change cataclysm). We drive around using crushed dinosaur parts. Iron is mostly a by-product of bacterial metabolism. So is oxygen. Mountains can be made of shells and fossilized bacteria. Death and the mesh go together in another sense, too, because natural selection implies extinction.[22]

Beings such as bees and flowers evolve together; all living beings evolve according to their environments.[23] But it would be wrong to claim that species look like they do because they are somehow "fitted" for their eco-logical niche. Darwin dispenses with the assumption that vultures are bald because they like sticking their heads into filth or that vines have hooks on them because they are useful for sticking on trees. Yes, those bald heads are handy for sticking into filth. But that isn't why they evolved.[24] The mesh must be made of very interesting material indeed. It isn't "organic," in the sense of form fitting function. William Wordsworth wanted to show how the organic world was "fitted" to the mind, and vice versa.[25] The theory of evolution, the basis of the ecological thought, does use words such as "fittest" and "adaptation," but it doesn't imply that bald heads exist because of piles of filth. Darwin would have concurred with the poet William Blake, who wrote in the margins of his copy of Wordsworth at those precise lines about fitting, "You shall not bring me down to believe such fitting & fitted . . . & please your lordship."[26] Natural selection isn't about decorum or an organic "fit." Coots don't have webbed feet, but they seem to do just fine in the water.[27] It was Alfred Russel Wallace who nervously persuaded Darwin to insert Herbert Spencer's invidious phrase "survival of the fittest" into *The Origin of Species*.[28] Wallace was concerned about the apparent pointlessness of life forms. For the ecological thought, this is their saving grace.

The mesh consists of infinite connections and infinitesimal differences. Few would argue that a single evolutionary change isn't minute.[29] Scale is infinite in both directions: infinite in size and infinite in detail. And each being in the mesh interacts with others. The mesh isn't static.[30] We can't rigidly specify anything as irrelevant. If there is no background and therefore no foreground, then where are we? We orient ourselves according to backgrounds against which we stand out. There is a word for a state without a foreground–background distinction: madness.

The ecological crisis makes us aware of how interdependent everything is. This has resulted in a creepy sensation that there is literally no world anymore. We have gained Google Earth but lost the world. "World" means a location, a background against which our actions become significant. But in a situation in which everything is potentially significant, we're lost. It's the same situation the schizophrenic finds herself in. She is unable to distinguish between information (foreground) and noise (background).[31] So she hears voices coming from the radiator, yet hears speech as meaningless burbling. Everything seems threateningly meaningful, but she can't pin down what the meaning is.

The more we become aware of the dangers of ecological instability—
extinctions, melting ice caps, rising sea levels, starvation—the more we find
ourselves lacking a reference point. When we think big we discover a hole
in our psychological universe. There is no way of measuring anything
anymore, since there is nowhere "outside" this universe from which to
take an impartial measurement. Strangely, thinking big doesn't mean that
we put everything in a big box. Thinking big means that the box melts into
nothing in our hands.

We're losing the very ground under our feet. In philosophical language, we're not just losing "ontological" levels of meaningfulness. We're
losing the "ontic," the actual physical level we trusted for so long. Imagine
all the air we breathe becoming unbreathable. There will be no more environmental poetry because we will all be dead. Some ecological language
appears to delight in this, even sadistically, by imagining what the world
would be like without us. Some deep ecological writing anticipates a day
when humans are obliterated like a toxic virus or vermin. Other texts
imagine "the day after tomorrow."[32] It's hard to be here right now. There
is some relief in picturing ourselves dead. I find this more than disturbing. Awareness of the mesh doesn't bring out the best in people. There is
a horrible bliss in becoming aware of what H. P. Lovecraft calls the fact
"that one is no longer a definite being distinguished from other beings."[33]
It's important not to panic and, strange to say, overreact to the tear in the
real. If it has always been there, it's not so bad, is it?

It gets worse, because we're losing the ground under our feet at the
exact same time as we're figuring out just how dependent upon that very
ground we are. We find ourselves pinned to the void. Schizophrenia is
a defense, a desperate attempt to restore a sense of solidity and consistency. It's highly likely that some environmental rhetoric is delusive in
this way. By reasserting a lost harmony with a lost lifeworld, this rhetoric tries desperately to paper over the crack. The paper itself betrays the
crack. Thinking big involves facing the meaninglessness and disorienting openness of the ecological thought.[34] Interconnectedness isn't snug
and cozy. There is intimacy, as we shall see, but not predictable, warm
fuzziness.

Do we fill the hole in the world with holism and Heidegger? Or do we
go all the way into the hole? Perhaps it's a benign hole: through it we might

glimpse the Universe. Many environmental writers tell us to "connect."[35] The issue is more about regrouping: reestablishing some functioning fantasy that will do for now, to preserve our sanity. Yet this is radically impossible, because of the total nature of the catastrophe and the fact that there is no script for it (we are "still here," and so on). It's like waking up: it becomes impossible to go back to sleep and dream in good faith. The ecological disaster is like being in a cinema when suddenly the movie itself melts. Then the screen melts. Then the cinema itself melts. Or you realize your chair is crawling with maggots. You can't just change the movie. Fantasizing at all becomes dubious.

Denying the problem, like the Bush administration of 2001–2008, amplifies the danger. And more subtle forms of denial exist. Wishing the problem away by "doing one's bit"—I use wartime rhetoric deliberately—is also avoiding the void. In the Second World War, British people hoarded tin cans to be made into aircraft and weapons. Whether or not the government really manufactured these products as a result, repetitive, compulsive activity kept horror at bay. Helpful as they are, recycling and other forms of individual and local action could also become ways of fending off the scope of the crisis and the vastness and depth of interconnectedness. These responses fit contemporary capitalist life. Being tidy and efficient is a good idea, but it isn't the meaning of existence. As Barack Obama memorably told his campaign staff in Fall 2008, " 'we can't solve global warming because I f——ing changed light bulbs in my house. It's because of something collective.' "[36]

There is, however, at least the satisfaction that one is finally taking charge of one's own shit, literally and figuratively. Psychoanalysis maintains that disposing of shit is the quintessential human problem. I beg to differ.[37] Still, what's interesting about recycling culture is that the mysterious curvature of social space-time, the curvature marked by the bend in the tube beneath the toilet bowl, disappears. We know where our shit goes. There are even some new pages about it in Richard Scarry's popular children's book *Busy, Busy Town*.[38] The lack of invisible places in our social space prevents us from separating public and private, local and global.[39] This was already the case in Tibet, where in charnel grounds outside the village the sky butcher chopped up your corpse to be eaten by the vultures, the ultimate ecological funeral.

Our situation is fascinatingly contradictory. On the one hand, we know more. On the other hand, this very knowledge means we lose touch with reality as we thought we knew it. We have more detail and more emptiness. The scope of our problem becomes clearer and clearer and more and more open and outrageous. It might be strictly impossible to draw a new map with new coordinates. The ecological thought has no center and no edge. Even if it were possible to find a center, would it be desirable? If all our previous forms of orientation, from the slingshot to the megaton bomb, from tribalism to totalitarianism, have contributed to the problem, shouldn't we be suspicious of finding our bearings too soon, even if we could?[40]

The more intense environmental awareness becomes, the more puzzling it grows, in a positive feedback loop. We may all now be experiencing what Thoreau wrote concerning the ascent of Mount Katahdin:

> What is it to be admitted to a museum, to see a myriad of particular things, compared with being shown some star's surface, some hard matter in its home! I stand in awe of my body, this matter to which I am bound here become so strange to me. I fear not spirits, ghosts, of which I am one . . . but I fear bodies, I tremble to meet them . . . Talk of mysteries! Think of our life in nature,—daily to be shown matter, to come into contact with it,—rocks, trees, wind on our cheeks! the *solid* earth! the *actual* world! the *common sense! Contact! Contact! Who* are we? *Where* are we?[41]

Thoreau's sense of actuality explodes as his sense of ground vanishes. The "hard matter in its home" is also the "surface" of "some star"—at once right *there* and somewhere, anywhere, else. The Romantic rush isn't so easy to appreciate today. We suppose either that Thoreau was a brave soul or that he was whistling in the dark. His language floats between both possibilities. Nowadays we're slightly surer of one thing. Yes, everything is interconnected. And it sucks.

LESS IS MORE: THINKING THE MESH

If everything is interconnected, there is less of everything. Nothing is complete in itself. Consider symbiosis. A tree includes fungi and lichen.

Lichen is two life forms interacting—a fungus and a bacterium or a fungus and an alga. Seeds and pollen have birds and bees to circulate them. Animal and fungal cells include mitochondria, energy cells (organelles) that are evolved bacteria taking refuge from a (for them) toxically oxygenated world. Plants are green (the color of Nature) because they contain chloroplasts, derived from the cyanobacteria. Mitochondria and chloroplasts have their own DNA and perform their own asexual reproduction. Our stomachs contain benign bacteria and harmless amoebae. Termites rely on bacteria and amoebae in their stomachs to break down cellulose; the termites live on the waste products. These mixotricha are themselves a "town" of tiny spirochetes resembling cilia (little waving hairs) and pill-shaped bacteria on the surface into which the spirochetes fit. Sponges are communities of protozoa; amoebae can form collective one-millimeter-long "slugs." The first "metazoan" was a colony of flagellate protozoa (tiny creatures with tiny tails). Most of the root hairs of plants are tiny fungi, the mycorrhizae. At the viral level, there are all kinds of replicating entities: "plasmids, episomes, insertion sequences, plasmons, virions, transposons, replicons, viruses."[42] And ultimately, as Richard Dawkins puts it, "we are all symbiotic colonies of genes."[43] Even DNA is subject to symbiosis, coevolution, parasitism, conflict, and cooperation.[44] We consist of organs without bodies, like the grin of the Cheshire cat.[45]

Symbiosis isn't the half of it. Dawkins's hypothesis of the "extended phenotype" is that DNA acts at a distance on organisms outside its particular vehicles (such as you and me). DNA's "genotype" expresses itself in the varied phenotypes of life. You are a phenotype; but so, in a way, is your house. A spider's web is a phenotype. Does the beaver phenotype stop at the end of its whiskers or at the end of a beaver's dam? Some kinds of animal saliva from chewing herbivores have profound effects on plants.[46] Snail shell size may well be a function of fluke genes, since the shell is a phenotype that snails share with their fluke parasites, just as a beaver couple shares a dam. Fluke genes will even influence snails lacking fluke parasites, appearing to control their behavior. Ti plasmids manipulate their bacterial hosts to enable trees to produce galls in which insects live. Meanwhile the plant tissue that generates the gall appears to have been produced for the sake of the insect. Shrimp are manipulated by flukes, which in turn manipulate the ducks that feed on the shrimp. When you sneeze, is it because a virus manipulated you to propagate its DNA? After all, rabid animals (even gentle ones) are possessed by an urge to bite. Some parasites and symbionts are so intimate you can't tell where one starts and its habitat stops, all the way down to the DNA level. There is no way of knowing which bits of our DNA are actually "ours" and which are plasmid insertions.[47] The human genome contains endogenous retrovirus derived sequences, and one of these, ERV-3, may confer immunosuppressive properties to the placenta, thus allowing embryos to coexist with the mother's body. Thus, that you are here today reading this is partly owing to a virus in your mother's DNA that may have prevented her from spontaneously aborting you.[48]

There is less substance: "Organisms and genomes may . . . be regarded as compartments of the biosphere through which genes in general circulate."[49] The ecological thought isn't about a superorganism. Holism maintains that the whole is greater than the sum of its parts. "Nature" tends to be holistic. Unlike Nature, what the ecological thought is thinking isn't more than the sum of its parts. Taxes are lower for married people because, in a sense, there is "less" of them than two individuals. If we want ecology, we will have to trade in Nature for something that seems more meager. The mesh is made of insubstantial stuff, and its structure is very strange. The more we examine it, the hollower it seems. Gaia is out. "Harmony" is out, but cooperation is in.[50]

Less is more. Darwin's thinking tries to imagine the "cheapest" way for organisms to evolve (the path of least resistance). Consider large testes in certain apes such as humans: if they don't rock the evolutionary boat, organs survive the way they are.[51] The ecological thought can't say what "nature" is. This doesn't (even) mean that "nature" is some mystical hyperthing beyond comprehension. Because evolution isn't linear, the mesh isn't bigger than the sum of its parts. There is no point in appealing to a "more than human world" as some writers put it.[52] So if everything is "less," if everything "doesn't really exist," will it not be hard to care about it? The ecological thought responds in the following ways. (1) When did things ever exist "more" than now? We care about them now, don't we? So what is the problem? (2) Since everything depends upon everything else, we have a very powerful argument for caring about things. The destruction of some things will affect other things. (3) What does "exist" mean?

If it means "exist independently," then why would something need our care? If it were all right by itself, thank you very much, why would we need to care for it?

On the one hand, our world expands as our knowledge grows. But on the other hand, it shrinks: things are "less" than we thought they were. We discover that our more detailed understanding of how things connect with each other results in a loss of a sense of reality. A void opens up in our social and psychological space. On the micro and macro levels, things are less complete, less integrated, less independent, than we believed.

The insides of organisms teem with aliens. As Lynn Margulis has shown, our cells contain the original bacteria, the Archæan anaerobic ones, the prokaryotes, hiding in organic tissue from the ecological disaster they created, the disaster called oxygen. This is the theory of endosymbiosis: symbiosis takes place within as well as among organisms. Exchange and interdependence occur at all levels. The surfaces of living beings are envelopes and filters, thick regions where complex chemical transfers and reactions take place. Biochemistry is only beginning to discover the precise mechanisms of photosynthesis and the transfer of nutrients across the placenta to the embryo. The interfaces involved host countless parasites and symbionts. At a microlevel, it becomes impossible to tell whether the mishmash of replicating entities are rebels or parasites: inside–outside distinctions break down.[53] The more we know, the less self-contained living beings become. Chemistry and physics discover how malleable and fungible things are, down to the tiniest nanoscale objects.[54] We dream about total manipulation. We could turn a piece of wood into a chunk of meat. Military nanotechnology now helps backpackers stay dry by pointing certain atoms in their pants in certain specific directions, thus causing liquids to leach out.

These dreams of abundance and control are tempered by knowledge itself, which asserts that nothing has intrinsic identity. Transgenic art contemplates this fact. Eduardo Kac's fluorescent rabbit, created with genes from a jellyfish, is the perfect example.[55] Is the horror of this art simply the shock value derived from the clichéd Frankenstein interpretation— that science has overstepped the bounds of human propriety? Or is it the revelation that if you can do that to a rabbit, then there wasn't that much of a rabbit in the first place? If you really could put duck genes in rabbit genes and rabbit genes in duck genes, it would give a new spin to Joseph Jastrow's duck–rabbit illusion. You really would be able to see a duck and a rabbit at the same time, because you really never saw a duck or a rabbit in the first place. There are less ducks and less rabbits not in number but in essence. We're faced with the extraordinary fact of increasing detail and vanishing fullness. The ecological thought makes our world vaster and more insubstantial at the same time.

We should be careful about ideas of meagerness and poverty. Environmentalism commonly finds them quite attractive. There is a "less is more" argument that ecological social policy is always about limits. You hear it frequently, especially when it comes to the fear that there are too many humans on Earth. This is one of the central platforms of deep ecology. It's a very suggestive idea, made more suggestive by a dash of Darwin and a pinch of Thomas Malthus.[56] When I lived in Colorado, I found the "Malthus was right" bumper stickers disturbing. Here we were, in the middle of nowhere—from my dense urban European perspective—worrying, basically, about immigrants spoiling our view. Conservatism and neoliberalism have used Darwin to justify welfare cuts, just as Malthus himself wrote his book on population to justify the British government slashing the welfare laws of his day. The model behind this justification is a view of limited, scarce resources. But Darwin's story is also one of proliferation, randomness, contingency, and useless display. The jungle isn't the concrete jungle. The theory of evolution transcends attempts to turn it into a theological defense of the status quo.[57]

Beyond the disturbing racism of the "population debate," what bothers me is that the language of limits edits questions of pleasure and enjoyment out of the ecological picture. Marx's criticism of capitalism wasn't so much that it's overrun with evil pleasures—the standard environmentalist view, as a glance at an almost progressive magazine such as *Adbusters* will confirm—but that it is nowhere near enjoyable enough. I'm not talking about the "right" of Big Oil to "enjoy" its massive profits at the expense of "the soil and the worker" (Marx's phrase).[58] I'm talking about how the language of curbs turns ecology into personal and interpersonal puritanism. If the ecological thought is about thinking big as much as or more than "small is beautiful," then it must explore and expand upon existing pleasures. If interconnectedness implies radical intimacy with other beings,

then we had better start thinking about pleasure as a coordinate of the
ecological thought. We must take a new path, into the vast mesh of interconnection. Who lives there?

STRANGE STRANGERS: THE POLITICS
AND POETICS OF COEXISTENCE

If we think the ecological thought, two things happen. Our perspective
becomes very vast. More and more aspects of the Universe become included in the ecological thought. At the same time, our view becomes
very profound. If everything is interconnected to everything, what exactly are the things that are connected? In some significant sense, if we
already know what they are, if we already have a box in which to put them,
they are not truly different beings. If the ecological thought is profound
as well as vast, we can't predict or anticipate just who or what—and can we
tell between "who" and "what," and how can we tell?—arrives at the inter-
sections in the unimaginably gigantic mesh. Individual beings become
more unique, even as they become more susceptible to measurement and
analysis.

Really thinking the mesh means letting go of an idea that it has a center. There is no being in the "middle"—what would "middle" mean anyway? The most important? How can one being be more important than
another? This creates problems for environmental ethics, which risks
oversimplifying things to coerce people to act. Movies about endangered
species tend to focus on one species at a time. From a penguin's point of
view, seals are dangerous monsters.[59] But from a seal's point of view, an
orca or a human with a club is the monster. The aesthetic of "cuteness"—a
rough version of Kantian beauty (it's small and perfectly formed and
doesn't hassle our mind)—might only be applicable to one species at a
time. A dog might look cute until it bites into a partridge's neck. When we
consider the mesh, we must drop this "one at a time" sequencing. So awareness of the mesh may suck the cuteness out of beings. Songs about the
mesh, such as "We Are All Earthlings" (from Sesame Street), may have it
wrong—they are about multitudes of cute creatures, and cuteness doesn't
come in multitudes.[60] (In Chapter 2, I discuss some exceptions to the problem of cuteness.)

If we keep thinking this "no center or edge" aspect of the mesh, we discover that there is no definite "within" or "outside" of beings. Everything is adapted to everything else.[61] This includes organs and the cells that constitute them. The mesh extends inside beings as well as among them. An organ that may have performed one function in one life form might now perform a different function in another one, or none at all. Then there is symbiosis. Margulis asserts that symbiosis is the fundamental driving force of evolution.[62] This also affects the rhetoric of cuteness. What is cute and cuddly about symbiosis? Even worse, what about endosymbiosis—the fact that our cells contain anaerobic bacteria, for example? It sounds more like monstrosity. Cuteness requires a minimum of integration.

Although there is no absolute, definite "inside" or "outside" of beings, we cannot get along without these concepts either. The mesh is highly paradoxical. Endosymbiosis abolishes inside–outside distinctions. A life form must have a boundary for filtering nutrients and poisons. Yet these boundaries are not perfectly defined. An oyster makes a pearl by secreting fluids around a piece of grit it has accidentally absorbed. Surgeons can transplant organs. The same thing occurs at larger scales. You only have to think of a coral reef to realize how life has influenced Earth; in fact, you only have to breathe, as oxygen is a by-product of the first Archæan beings (from 2.5 billion years ago back to an undefined limit after the origin of Earth 4.5 billion years ago). The hills are teeming with the skeletal silence of dead life forms.

The ecological thought permits no distance. Thinking interdependence involves dissolving the barrier between "over here" and "over there," and more fundamentally, the metaphysical illusion of rigid, narrow boundaries between inside and outside.[63] Thinking interdependence involves thinking difference. This means confronting the fact that all beings are related to each other negatively and differentially, in an open system without center or edge. In a language, a word means what it means because of its difference with other words. There is nothing intrinsic to the word that makes it mean what it means. The same goes for how it sounds.[64] The mesh is also made of negative difference, which means it doesn't contain positive, really existing (independent, solid) things. This should be an utterly mind-blowing idea, so don't worry if you're having trouble imagining it. Consider Indra's net, used in Buddhist scripture to describe interdependence: "At every connection in this infinite net hangs a magnificently polished and infinitely faceted jewel, which reflects in each of its facets all the facets of every other jewel in the net. Since the net itself, the number of jewels, and the facets of every jewel are infinite, the number of reflections is infinite as well."[65]

What we're examining here is that scary thing, "totality." Recent thinkers have been shy of totality.[66] They fear that totality means totalitarianism. Totality may be difficult and frightening. But the current global crisis requires that we wake up and smell the total coffee. It's strictly impossible to equate this total interconnectedness, Indra's net, with something beyond us or larger than us. Total interconnectedness isn't holistic. We're definitely not talking about totalitarianism, and we're not talking about large things as opposed to small ones. Indra's net implies that large and small things, near and far things, are all "near." "Totality" doesn't mean something closed, single, and independent, nor does it mean something predetermined and fixed; it has no goal.

Very large finitude is harder to deal with than an abstract, ideal infinity.[67] As I noted in the Introduction, it might be harder to imagine four and a half billion years than abstract eternity. It might be harder to imagine evolution than to imagine abstract infinity. Actuality presents us with disturbingly large finitudes. Quantity humiliates.[68] The other appears in this world, not beyond it.[69] Face it we must. Perhaps "untotality" would express it better, but we don't need to invent clever ways of saying the same thing. Think big, then bigger still—beyond containment, beyond the panoramic spectacle that dissolves everything within itself.[70]

The mesh is vast yet intimate: there is no here or there, so everything is brought within our awareness. The more we analyze, the more ambiguous things become. We can't really know who is at the junctions of the mesh before we meet them. Even when we meet them, they are liable to change before our eyes, and our view of them is also labile. These beings are the *strange stranger*. You won't see references to animals in this book except in quotation marks. You will see absolutely no references to "the animal" or, even worse, to "the animal question," as some contemporary philosophers put it (have they forgotten the resonance of "the Jewish question"?). Might this "question" be a product of a capitalist age, in which, as Marx comments, money is removed from other commodities and made to stand for commodity-ness as such, as if "there existed *the* Animal, the individual incarnation of the entire animal kingdom"?[71] Could treating people like "animals" result from this alienating abstraction?

Saying "Humans are animals" could get you in trouble. So could saying "Humans are not animals," for different reasons. The word "animal" shows how humans develop intolerances to strangeness and to the stranger. According to prevailing ideologies, we must become, or be thought of as, like "animals" (biocentrism), or they should become, or be thought of as, like us (anthropocentrism). Neither choice is satisfactory. There is no way to maintain the strangeness of things. Equating humans with "animals" seems right. But "animals" are often shorthand for tools or objects of instrumental reason—the equation doesn't sound so clever when you put it that way. Humans are like "animals," but "animals" are not "animals," as we are beginning to see.

We should instead explore the paradoxes and fissures of identity *within* "human" and "animal." Instead of "animal," I use *strange stranger*. This stranger isn't just strange. She, or he, or it—can we tell? how?—is strangely strange. Their strangeness itself is strange.[72] We can never absolutely figure them out. If we could, then all we would have is a ready-made box to put them in, and we would just be looking at the box, not at the strange strangers. They are intrinsically strange. Do we know for sure whether they are sentient or not? Do we know whether they are alive or not? Their strangeness is part of who they are.[73] After all, they might be us. And what could be stranger than what is familiar? As anyone who has a long-term partner can attest, the strangest person is the one you wake up with every morning. Far from gradually erasing strangeness, intimacy heightens it. The more we know them, the stranger they become. Intimacy itself is strange. As the passenger side-view mirror on your car reads, "Objects in mirror are closer than they appear." We ignore the mesh because we're so familiar with it.[74] Our familiarity forms the basis of the threatening intimacy that we too often push to the backs of our minds.

Imagine living in a world of triangular creatures. A triangular scientist discovers creatures without angles. These "smooth strangers" would be "strange" only insofar as we don't usually encounter them in our world. But we can imagine such a creature. And if one ever showed up, it would be a "familiar stranger"—we would have anticipated its existence. We would need some time, of course, to get to know its smoothness. But this process would be finite. The strange stranger, conversely, is something or someone whose existence we cannot anticipate. Even when strange strangers showed up, even if they lived with us for a thousand years, we might never know them fully—and we would never know whether we had exhausted our getting-to-know process. We wouldn't know what we did not know about them—these aspects would be unknown unknowns, in the inimitable phrasing of the U.S. secretary of defense who in 2003 promoted a disastrous war.[75] They might be living with us right now. They might, indeed, be us. That is what is so strange about them. We can never tell.

Most philosophers (excepting Peter Singer and other utilitarians) opt out of including animals on "this" side of things. Sensing the danger of excluding them from ethics, Emmanuel Levinas, fearless thinker of our infinite obligations to others, grudgingly includes some "animals" within his idea of the "face," his term for the *thisness* and presence of the actual other person—"the infinite which blinks."[76] The closer you look, the weirder strange strangers become. Let's examine them in detail, starting with a consideration of time—evolution. There are two main levels: the growth and death of life forms, and the history of evolution as such. We shall travel through a discussion of time, take a detour through Samuel Taylor Coleridge's poem *The Rime of the Ancient Mariner*, then return.

Ecology isn't only about vast space but also about vast time. Ecological time and geological time are difficult to grasp intuitively. Vast time opened up in the Romantic period, when people such as Mary Anning discovered the first dinosaur fossils, and the geologist Charles Lyell began to establish just how ancient Earth really is.[77] Life on Earth wasn't just thousands but millions of years old, and Earth itself was therefore even older. The concept of "prehistory" vanishes as we think the ecological thought. The whole thing is history.[78] What we call Nature is really just solidified history that we aren't studying closely enough. But it's arduous to think of time on Earth as historical all the way back. The time of evolution is almost inconceivably slow. Think of those wonderfully displacing 1970s television documentaries such as Carl Sagan's *Cosmos*, which depict humans arriving on the scene at a minute to midnight, or a second to midnight, in a metaphor that depicts the time of Earth or the universe as a single day, a month, or a year. But even the time of living and dying takes a stretch of the imagination. There must be some way of helping us to visualize it.

Think of a time-lapse movie: the camera records a flower growing from a bud, opening, aging, withering, and finally shedding its petals. We have only to speed up our sense of time to see how strange life forms are. They arise, flicker, and vanish. Plants and fungi do move, like animals in slow motion (think of a sunflower). If you read Darwin, the strongest thing you take away is a feeling of time-lapse. Each species is like a river; rivers join and part without much regard for boundaries. Rivers flow, so we can never talk about the "same" river, only river stages.[79] A species is like that. Evolution is like that. Species and individual members of a species are like the flowing flames of flowers discovered in time-lapse animation. The ancient Greek philosopher Heraclitus was right to assert that *panta rhei*, "Everything flows."

By speeding up the world, time-lapse photography makes things that seem natural reveal something monstrous or artificial, an uncanny, morphing flow. This flow has been ongoing since DNA started its random mutations. Evolution is mutagenic. It isn't linear or progressive. If you threw up a "handful of feathers . . . all must fall to the ground according to definite laws; but how simple is this problem compared to the action and reaction of the innumerable plants and animals which have determined, in the course of centuries, the proportional numbers and kinds of trees now growing on the old Indian ruins [in the southern United States]!"[80] These interactions have produced, and are producing, all the life forms we see today.[81]

If we sped up evolution like a time-lapse movie, we would notice many strange things. The eye has evolved no less than forty separate times.[82] DNA code contains thousands of repeated or possibly redundant strings of information. You can inject fresh pieces of gene in a modified virus directly into the cells at the back of the eye to improve eyesight.[83] DNA isn't a blueprint—it's more like a recipe, and recipes can produce very different results.[84] Thankfully, living organisms are not designed, and there is no "intelligence" behind the mutation—unless by "design" we mean the processes of evolution: adaptation, selection, and variation, carrying on through hundreds of millions of years in a highly distributed fashion. No one special being is uniquely responsible for the existence of future beings.[85]

Time-lapse makes things appear unnatural: even flowers take on a weird, monstrous quality. This unnaturalness speaks a truth of evolution itself. Life forms didn't evolve holistically, and they didn't evolve with a "point" (telos): there is nothing inevitable in evolution. If you could see evolution happening rapidly, you wouldn't be tempted to say something like, "Look at those wings: how perfectly developed for flying through the sky." Not all water birds have webbed feet. Like a horror movie, evolution is as much about disintegration as it is about things coming together. Naturalness is a temporal illusion: like seasons, things seem static because we don't notice them changing, and when they do change, there is a rough predictability to the way they do so. Horror and disgust arise whenever that neat aesthetic frame breaks. In this ecological age, we must take stock of these unaesthetic reactions—acknowledging, for example, the rapid mutagenic effects of radiation.

Many parts of life forms serve no function whatsoever. They just evolved. Darwin discusses vestigial and rudimentary organs in *The Descent of Man*. Your ears do not have to be the shape they are: think of a cell phone microphone (just a pinprick hole). Ears are shaped in that spiraling, shell-like way because they are made of cartilage stiff enough to enable you to prick up your ears properly, which you don't, of course, because you're human—unless you do (some people can and do prick up their ears, as Darwin notes).[86] See the problem? That little bump on the inside upper flap of your ear is a vestige of pointed ears turned inward.[87] Our cranial nerves are derived from the gill arches of fish.[88] A life form flows around within its unstable liquid environment in a highly metamorphic way. If you trace the history of evolution backward, you will see no rhyme or reason to it—well, you will see a great deal of incredible rhyme and intricate reason but no progress (no teleology) and no climax. Humans are not some mysterious "Omega point," as one Christian evolutionist claimed.[89] Humans are not the culmination of anything; they aren't even *a* culmination of anything. All that we call Nature is mutation and often pointless—thinking otherwise is called "adaptationism."[90] Evolution shares pointlessness with art, which at bottom is vague and purposeless.[91] There is no really good reason for it. In fact, some organisms, from butterflies to apes, capitalize on pointless mutations in the process of sexual selection. This was one reason why Marx thought that Darwin was very helpful to materialism. If you could get past the stuffy Anglo-empiricism, you would find a convincing refutation of the notion of teleology, the idea that things have a point: "Not only is a death blow dealt here for the first time to 'Teleology' in the natural sciences but their rational meaning is empirically explained."[92]

How pointless is evolution? DNA mutates randomly. Mutations are random with respect to current need, a conclusion Darwin drew himself. If you drop a mouse into a colder climate than she is used to, her descendants won't necessarily grow warmer coats in order to "adapt." What does this mean? It means, profoundly, that there is no environment as such. Mice don't evolve warm coats "in order to" accommodate themselves to an environment. It may just so happen that mice with warmer coats survive. But it would be a mistake—the mistake called adaptationism—to think that this means that they evolved "in order to" adapt to their environment.

A time-lapse film of a flower growing and dying shows not only its fragility and unique beauty but also its linkage with everything else. When the flower becomes like a flame that spurts, flickers, and dies in a few seconds, we see it less as a solid single lasting thing. The time-lapse view is what makes Coleridge's poem *The Rime of the Ancient Mariner* such a powerful ecological statement. Unlike Wordsworth's poems in the groundbreaking *Lyrical Ballads*, Coleridge's poem is deliberately, relentlessly supernatural and uncanny. This could be better for the ecological thought than "realistic" writing. For Coleridge, "supernatural" meant super natural, like those tubes of toothpaste that say "30 percent extra"; extra Nature, more than you bargained for:

The ship was cheered, the harbour cleared,
Merrily did we drop
Below the kirk, below the hill,
Below the light-house top.

The sun now rose upon the left
Out of the sea came he

And he shone bright, and on the right
Went down into the sea.   (1.21–28)[93]

In just eight lines, the ship disappears over the horizon, and the sailors
can no longer see their homeland—they have left their world. The sun rises
and sets—a day passes in twenty-six words. Events rush like a waterfall.
We put our habitual way of being in time in a box and call it natural.
Coleridge shows Nature leaking out of the box. What a great poem to read
in a time of ecological emergency.

Don't shoot albatrosses! Is this really the moral of *The Rime of the Ancient Mariner?* Senseless violence against animals is wrong—so perhaps
sensible violence against them is justifiable? When the Mariner enjoins us
to love "All things both great and small" (7.615), he leaves the Wedding
Guest mind-blown, as if the bottom has dropped out of his world (7.622–
625). Is that really the reaction we would expect from such a trite sentiment? Even by the late eighteenth century, it was trite.

Coleridge's critique of sensibility is directed toward creating the potential for a radical democracy that transcends the politics of pity. The
moral of *The Ancient Mariner* can't possibly be not to shoot albatrosses.
The moral is about the traumatic encounter between strange strangers.
One of these, without a doubt, is the albatross itself; another is the Mariner, the zombie-like walking, talking poem; another, the Wedding Guest;
the Nightmare Life-in-Death; and several million water snakes, lowly
worms indeed. Coleridge brilliantly imagines the proximity the strange
stranger, who emerges from, and is, and constitutes, the environment.
The background becomes the foreground. It's the sheer "thereness," the
frightening presence of the Mariner himself, and the snakes that surround
the dead ship at the dead center of the poem.[94] It's the holy otherness of the
albatross, not the fact that it is a cute creature, great or small, which disturbs. The sailors can't fit it into their horizon of meaning, can't figure out
whether to blame it for the "fog and mist" (2.102).

The ecological thought consists in intimacy with the strange stranger.
We can't ever predict exactly who or what strange strangers are, whether
they are a "who" or a "what." If we can, then we are still clinging to a rei-
fied concept of Nature, whether it's the old school version or some new
and improved version. When the Mariner looks at the water snakes, he is

not, as he says, "Alone, alone, all all alone" (4.232). He is coexisting with
other beings that "liv[e] on": "And a thousand thousand slimy things /
Liv'd on; and so did I" (4.239–240). Darwin argues that human sympathy
derives from the basic social instincts of other sentient beings.[95] He provides many examples of nonhumans acting with seeming sympathy. What
the Mariner learns is how true sympathy comes from social feeling—the
awareness of coexistence.

The ecological thought needs to develop an ethical attitude we might
call "coexistentialism."[96] The Mariner hails the albatross, then the sailors
"hulloo" it like a hunting dog, then the Mariner shoots it like prey. There
is a descent in this progression. If we regard the albatross, the churning
sea "like a witch's oils" (2.129), the frightful, viral face ("as white as lep-
rosy"; 3.192) of "Life-in-Death" (3.193), and the water snakes (4.273–281)
as four modes of the same encounter, we witness the Mariner ignoring
the ethical entanglement with the other, then restarting it (or letting it
restart) from an unimaginably nightmarish ground. The disturbing, inert passivity of life forms is the zero level of this encounter. This "feminine" inertia is the ground of coexistentialism.[97] What we encounter in
the face of the female Life-in-Death isn't some utterly hostile violence
but a sickened hunger and vulnerability, whose very presence condemns
us: " 'The game is done! I've won, I've won!' / Quoth she, and whistles
thrice"—her strange vocalization is uncanny, inhuman (3.197–198). "Life-
in-Death" is a pretty good description of a virus. Coleridge confronts
us with the disturbingly non-thin, nonrigid boundary between life and
nonlife.

Interconnection implies separateness and difference. There would be no
mesh if there were no strange strangers.[98] The mesh isn't a background
against which the strange stranger appears. It is the entanglement of all
strangers. Consider some poetry concerning strangers. At his most vision-
ary, William Wordsworth loses his vision. The epiphanies in his master-
work, *The Prelude*, involve blanking out. Just like our experience of identity
in the mesh, these "spots of time" are often "less than" what the reader is
expecting. Wordsworth's loss of bearings is common in traumatic experiences. When you're in a car crash, time seems to slow down, even stop; everything seems unreal. In such moments, Wordsworth experiences himself as
the strange stranger. Then there are the people Wordsworth meets. Like

Coleridge's Ancient Mariner, these arrivals are unexpected. The encounter with the strange stranger breaks the cycle of sameness.

Wordsworth's particular genius is in seeing the environment incarnated in a unique person. The environment includes human history. Wordsworth is one of the greatest war poets, partly because the disturbing subtlety of his war references creeps up on us, like a figure emerging from a distance. "Old Man Travelling; Animal Tranquillity and Decay, a Sketch" suggestively links the human and "animal" realms. The poem resembles an excerpt from a picaresque novel. Perhaps the ecological thought is picaresque—wandering from place to place, open to random encounters.

> The little hedge-row birds,
> That peck along the road, regard him not.
> He travels on, and in his face, his step,
> His gait, is one expression; every limb,
> His look and bending figure, all bespeak
> A man who does not move with pain, but moves
> With thought—He is insensibly subdued
> To settled quiet: he is one by whom
> All effort seems forgotten, one to whom
> Long patience has such mild composure given,
> That patience now doth seem a thing, of which
> He hath no need. He is by nature led
> To peace so perfect, that the young behold
> With envy, what the old man hardly feels.
> —I asked him whither he was bound, and what
> The object of his journey; he replied
> "Sir! I am going many miles to take
> A last leave of my son, a mariner,
> Who from a sea-fight has been brought to Falmouth,
> And there is dying in an hospital."[99]

The way the line "The little hedgerow birds" hangs in space—incomplete, accidental—wonderfully suggests the contemplative quiet that settles over this poem. We're looking at the old man from the point of view of someone who sees the birds not "regarding" (line 2)—they remain uncon-

cerned that a human is passing. This image of unseeing is far more pro-
saic than Milton's imagery and more haunting. The narrator is in wonder
about the birds as much as about the old man.

The birds "peck along the road" (2)—"peck along" suggests tiny movements, something halfway between tiptoeing and nibbling, and something to do with thinking, which the old man's gait also conveys. "Peck
along" evokes "chew over." We can't resist the slightly creepy conclusion
that there is almost no one there.[100] What is remarkable about the old
man is how unremarkable he is. He isn't even remarkable to himself—"He
is insensibly subdued / To settled quiet" (7–8). "Subdued" suggests being
beaten down, the posture of a loser, but not an extraordinary loss, at least
not at this point in the poem. The old man has given up. He is unaware of
how he appears in the eyes of the other, in the envious "young" (14). The
poem shows us how the strange stranger can be strange in his ordinari-
ness, surprising in his mildness and passivity. The poem is pregnant with
thought, and finally with grief, for the old man is going to visit his dying
son. This isn't the only Wordsworth poem in which grief emerges from a
sustained engagement with an environment.

The big picture in the poem is that war is environmental—it seeps into
everything, even into the sight of an old man treading down a country
lane. Wordsworth is one of the most powerful antiwar poets of all time,
precisely because he writes about war in a sidelong way. Rather than pre-
senting full frontal violence, he shows how war is everywhere: we see it on
the television in our living room, we read it in the paper lying on the drive-
way, we feel it in the quiet tread of the old man. War is displacement in
multiple dimensions: the son who dies before the father, the people sent to a
foreign land, the way a "Nature poem" becomes a war poem. Isn't this why
ecological art must learn from the art of wartime? In a global environmental
emergency, there is no safe place. Ordinary things like birds pecking along a
road become pregnant with larger significance.

War is also about the unexpected encounter. "Strange Meeting" is Wilfred Owen's poem about a British soldier meeting a German one in a weird
space between life and death. In Wordsworth's poem, something apparently simple, inevitable, and obvious becomes strange, intimate, and painful. The ecological thought demands that we encounter the strange stranger
on many levels and on many scales: from the bacteria in our gut to birds

slick with oil to displaced victims of a hurricane. At the same time that we awaken to the ecological catastrophe that has already occurred, we're waking up to the fact that there was no Nature, no ground beneath our ontological feet. This is war, from the viewpoint of the weak and the indigent. This is realizing that we're always already responsible for the other.[101]

The old man in Wordsworth's poem emerges as if from a background of which he is part, a background of unconscious coexistence (the birds "regard him not"; 2). It's like the moment in the film *Contact* where Jodi Foster's character Dr. Arroway meets the alien—the environment shimmers and the figure of a man emerges in a "strange distortion."[102] When the environment becomes intimate—as it is in our age of ecological panic— it no longer remains an environment. The seemingly smooth transition of the poem as it flows down the page, in Wordsworth's beautifully open blank verse, belies the torsion and distortion of those final words about the dying son. In the same way, the ecological thought creeps over us to deliver a message of unbearable intimacy.

THE POETICS OF ANYWHERE

The strange stranger affects ideas of place and space. The essence of the local isn't familiarity but the uncanny, the strangely familiar and familiarly strange. The experience of the local is the profound experience of strangeness. Any poem by John Clare, an actual peasant, will satisfy your curiosity. Mull over the first line of "Autumn Birds": "The wild duck startles like a sudden thought."[103] The mind and the world it perceives are there, all at once, but not as a nice, integrated, "fitting" whole. Who is startling whom? Think of the baby mice in "Mouse's Nest," disturbingly alive in their extended phenotype of glistening pools:

> When out an old mouse bolted in the wheat
> With all her young ones hanging at her teats
> She looked so odd and so grotesque to me.
>
> (5–7)

The absolute "thereness" of the location stops you dead, at the same time as it leaves you high and dry: "The water o'er the pebbles scarce could run /

And broad old sexpools glittered in the sun" (13–14).[104] The Edenic local, by contrast, is a cheap imitation, the product of a society that displaces itself, that produces not just space junk but also *junkspace*. "Junkspace" is architect Rem Koolhaas' term for how space itself becomes part of the junk of a throwaway culture.[105]

Levinas evokes the "thereness of location" hauntingly when he refers to environments as "the element": "One is steeped in it."[106] Yet although Levinas says, "The element separates us from the infinite," it might be the platform for coexistentialism.[107] Levinas appears to concur when he describes "naked" existence as "not entirely absorbed in [the] form [of things]. . . . They are always in some respect like those industrial cities where everything is adapted to a goal of production, but which, full of smoke, full of wastes and sadness, exist also for themselves. For a thing nudity is the surplus of its being over its finality."[108] In modern junkspace, there is more infinity. As Andrei Tarkovsky understands in his intimate panning shots over pools full of detritus, waste and pollution are the face of the infinite (for Tarkovsky himself, the face of God). Levinas is profoundly ecological when he asserts, "A thing exists in the midst of its wastes."[109] Junkspace reveals this fact in a naked way.

We must therefore examine a different form of the strange stranger—the environment. Strange strangers are all around us, so let's consider this "all around" quality. Environments are made up of strange strangers. The phenotype produced by the genetic genotype includes the environment, like a beaver's dam or a mouse's nest.[110] Environments coevolve with organisms.[111] The world looks the way it looks because of life forms. The environment doesn't "exist" apart from them. The philosopher Georges Bataille had a suggestive phrase for "animal" existence: it's like "water in water."[112] The last parts of *The Origin of Species* show that climate, environment, and place are not strong determinants of living beings. Contrary to the beliefs of German Romantic thinkers such as Humboldt and Herder, there is no special "environment" separate from living organisms that somehow conditions their qualities. This belief in a special environment is a symptom of nationalism, and it's time to drop it. The ecological thought cannot abide national boundaries. This is another good thing about "Tibetans in space": nomads would never have developed ideas like Humboldt's and Herder's.

Sigmund Freud's essay "The Uncanny" is essential for thinking the ecological thought. The uncanny exists because we're always somewhere. Repetition, with its play of familiarity and difference, is thus possible. Freud's examples of being lost in a forest or a city, and of repeatedly returning to the same spot, emerge because of the existence of environments such as forests and cities:

> [A] recurrence of the same situations, things, and events . . . awaken[s] an uncanny feeling, which recalls that sense of helplessness sometimes experienced in dreams. Once, as I was walking through the deserted streets of a provincial town in Italy which was strange to me, on a hot summer afternoon, I found myself in a quarter the character of which could not long remain in doubt. Nothing but painted women were to be seen at the windows of the small houses, and I hastened to leave the narrow street at the next turning. But after having wandered about for a while . . . I suddenly found myself back in the same street, where my presence was now beginning to excite attention. I hurried away once more, but only to arrive yet a third time by devious paths in the same place. Now, however, a feeling overcame me which I can only describe as uncanny, and I was glad enough to abandon my exploratory walk and get straight back to the piazza. . . . Other situations having in common with my adventure an involuntary return to the same situation . . . also result in the same feeling of helplessness and of something uncanny. As, for instance, when one is lost in a forest in high altitudes, caught . . . by the mountain mist, and when every endeavor to find the marked or familiar path ends again and again in a return to one and the same spot, recognizable by some particular landmark.[113]

Here is shot through with *there*. Our sense of place includes a sense of difference. When we think the qualities (or lack thereof) of uncanny place, we arrive at a strangely familiar location—*anywhere*. Modern capitalism has turned America into a country of anywheres (Anytowns, U.S.A.). Neither nowhere nor everywhere, anywhere is a zero degree of place, hardly a location at all. Consider Freud's suggestive phrase, "that sense of helplessness sometimes experienced in dreams." Cities and forests are like dreams because they are autonomous: they have their own laws, their own movement. Strange strangers inhabit them. Even on a very superficial level, we can tell someone lives in the streets that are desolate for now, the forest that seems empty for now.

Isn't there something creepy about how the desolate streets, the empty forests, seem to become entities in themselves? It's like what Wordsworth describes in the "boat stealing" episode of *The Prelude*. As the boy Wordsworth paddles away from a mountain peak, parallax seems to make it loom larger, as if it were following him:

> my Boat
> Went heaving through the water, like a Swan;
> When from behind that craggy Steep, till then
> The bound of the horizon, a huge Cliff,
> As if with voluntary power instinct,
> Upreared its head. I struck, and struck again,
> And, growing still in stature, the huge Cliff
> Towered up between me and the stars, and still,
> With measured motion, like a living thing,
> Strode after me.   **(1.403–412)**

Isn't this the essence of ecological awareness? There is something sinister about discovering the mesh. It's as if there is something else—someone else, even—but the more we look, the less sure we are. It's uncanny: there is something there, and there isn't. Any form of ecological language that has a tin ear for this weirdness isn't worth the candle.

Why now? The uncanny stirs because total interconnectedness enables it. Industry means repetition, automation, and the creation of junkspace. Repetition and automation apply to the creation of spaces, not just the manufacture of objects. Think of a grid pattern of streets: functional, efficient, and easy to produce. A grid involves repetition in at least two dimensions—three if you include repeating tower blocks. You will inevitably encounter repetition in the modern city. You will inevitably experience the uncanny. The uncanny is a function of repetition, because it brings to light our compulsion to repeat, a feature of our psyche. This is why doppelgängers are uncanny and why the strange stranger in general is uncanny—both remind us of us. And people live in those streets—other people. Modern life multiplies these uncanny experiences.[114] The uncanny applies to evolution at large, because it appears to reenact its past actions.[115] The double walls of certain cells are evidence of some ancient coexistence.[116]

Since our psyche is always disturbing—it takes so long to contruct one, and there are so many rules for its construction—it is disquieting to see an image of our psyche in the external world, in the form of repeating patterns. It's our own artificiality, projected onto the outside world. The repetition involves an uneasy sense of emptiness: visualize the paintings of the surrealist Giorgio De Chirico—empty streets contain some unseen oppressive force, open doorways wait for us to enter them—or not—and streets not taken looking just like the streets we took. One of his titles says it all: *Mystery and Melancholy of a Street*. The "of" applies to the street itself. It's as if the streets and doorways are gazing at us. Modern life multiplies these experiences. The lyrics by Robert Smith (of The Cure) about being lost in a forest, looking for a girl, are disturbingly ecological: "The girl was never there, it's always the same / Running towards nothin', again and again and again and again" (23–24).[117] They convey the sense of environmental creepiness, of the environment as creepy, which overwhelms those now useless weather conversations.

The more ecological awareness we have, the more we experience the uncanny. Any environmentalism that edits this out is incomplete. If there is an inevitable experiential dimension of ecology, there is an inevitable psychological dimension. This psychological dimension includes weird phenomena that warp our psychic space. There is no smooth, flat, immediate ecological experience. It's all curved. Not acknowledging this aspect of ecological awareness is inaccurate and unrealistic at least, perhaps even dangerous. If we don't take the uncanny into account, we will just be trying to squeeze into a mold we don't really fit. This could have serious political consequences. Consider the idea of the "authoritarian personality," the too-normal person who seems to have purged herself or himself of negativity, perhaps of any trace of inner life—but at what cost?[118] Corporate culture selects for authoritarian personalities all the way down the chain of command. For the authoritarian personality, all psychic space appears smooth, spick and span. An ecological variant could easily arise.

Just as John Ashbery's poems are written for and about *anybody* (rather than everyman), so the ecological thought thinks place as *anywhere*.[119] Milton imagines "anywhere" in *Paradise Lost*, when Raphael envisions a possible extraterrestrial Eden. The idea of authentic place is a powerful Western myth, but indigenous cultures have traditions that include outer space. Nomadic Tibetan culture imagines meditation being practiced in other worlds and in other galaxies. The ecological thought must extend our sense of location to include "anywheres." "Anywhere" corrodes our sense of "here." Other times and other places are part of this "here." The more we study it, the more holes we find.

Imagine a line. Now remove the middle third. You have two shorter lines with an equal-sized space between them. Now remove the middle thirds of the two lines you have left. Keep going. You are creating a Cantor set. The mathematician Georg Cantor discovered it in the 1880s. The Cantor set contains an infinite number of points. Yet it also contains an infinite number of no-points. It appears to contain two different infinities. Does this make it weirdly larger than "regular" infinity? Cantor got into trouble for these thoughts. But his discoveries laid the foundations for set theory, Gödel's Incompleteness Theorem, and Alan Turing's thinking on artificial intelligence. It was also the basis of fractal geometry, which underlies the geometry of branching and circulatory systems in life forms.

This is Cantor dust: infinite dust and infinite no-dust. A three-dimensional version is called a Menger sponge, a fractal entity with infinity spaces and infinity points. Talk about holding infinity in the palm of your hand. You can't squeeze a Menger sponge. But there is something there. The Menger sponge is infinity on "this" side of phenomena. Gilles Deleuze describes Leibniz's view of matter, which is quite Menger-spongy: "Matter thus offers an infinitely porous, spongy or cavernous texture without emptiness, caverns endlessly contained in other caverns: no matter how small each body contains a world pierced with irregular passages, surrounded by an increasingly vaporous fluid, the totality of the Universe resembling a 'pond of matter in which there exist different flows and waves.'"[120] The strange stranger and "anywhere" are like the Menger sponge.

Recent time-lapse movies using NASA's Earth Observatory show the Amazon basin disappearing: years of activity compressed into ten seconds.

When you can see like this, the reality of our ecological disaster becomes vividly real, and at the same time, the literal ground disappears before our very eyes.[121] Learning about global warming serves to make us feel something much worse than an existential threat to our lifeworld. It forces us to realize that there never was a lifeworld in the first place, that in a sense "lifeworld" was an optical illusion that depended on our not seeing the extra dimension that NASA, Google Earth, and global warming mapping open up. The more information we acquire in the greedy pursuit of seeing everything, the more our sense of a deep, rich, coherent world will appear unavailable: it will seem to have faded into the past (nostalgia) or to belong only to others (primitivism). Some of us will eventually think that we once inhabited this deep, rich, lost world. Others will realize that even this sense of loss is an illusion created by our current modes of seeing. We could read the recently discovered phallic symbols drawn on unsuspecting householders' roofs, symbols that can be seen only with the aid of Google Earth, as desperate, impotent attempts to normalize a situation that borders on psychosis, through crude Freudian humor.[122]

A place bounded by a horizon now seems a mere patch. That is why the really evocative poetry of place is mysterious and uncanny. There is an awareness that "here" already includes "elsewhere," that "here" is "anywhere." One of the most vividly imagined narratives of "anywhere" is Kim Stanley Robinson's masterpiece, the Mars trilogy (*Red Mars*, *Green Mars*, and *Blue Mars*). Humans arrive and "terraform" Mars, slowly introducing a breathable atmosphere, water, and plant life. At every stage they must make conscious decisions. Nothing is given. Humans must create the backdrop for their historical dramas. There is no Nature. Everything is artificial. This means that, at the beginning at least, almost anywhere on Mars is as good (or as poor) as anywhere else. The Mars trilogy shows how the ecological thought must include social theory and social practice.

Earth is under terrible stress in Robinson's novels. To relieve the stress, global corporations start doing what they have done on Earth: undertaking colonialism and imperialism. There was always a planetary scale to this project in any case. Queen Elizabeth I's letter establishing the first English global corporation, the East India Company, declared that the purpose of international trade is to knit nations closer together.[123] Colonialism tells stories of a fabulous, mythical realm "over yonder" that provides a jackpot of enjoyment, a constant drizzle of luxuries. Some of the first language of global environmental awareness was capitalist poetry, the advertising language of big commerce from about 1650 to about 1800. The only thing Robinson adds is the terraforming. Even that was present in the way colonialism created monocultures, ecological disaster areas that grew only one crop, like Ireland, where the potato monoculture eventually resulted in a devastating famine. Certain places were known only for the commodities they grew—consider the "Spice Islands."[124]

The fun begins on Mars when some colonists decide that they want to cut loose from the oppressive colonial structure. This involves violence. Whatever the colonists do, they are burdened with the full knowledge that they are shaping a world. In deciding to flood Mars with water, the rebel colonists have simply decided to live. A religious splinter group splits from the rebel group. The group values Mars as its own place, as a unique entity. A conflict emerges between "red" Martians, who want to retain an original, authentic Mars, and "green" Martians, who don't.

A marvelous passage at the beginning of *Green Mars* describes how the planet itself is part of the terraforming project. The narrator imagines how the formation of Mars for human habitation cannot replicate that of Earth: "all the genetic templates for our new biota are Terran; the minds designing them are Terran; but the terrain is Martian. And terrain is a powerful genetic engineer, determining what flourishes and what doesn't, pushing along progressive differentiation, and thus the evolution of new species."[125] In this sense, the background is never just a background. The very planet the humans terraform dictates what lives and what dies, shaping the forces of evolution. The planet itself is a "genetic engineer." It has as much input as any other actor, maybe more. To this extent, we are indeed all Earthlings. Heidegger poetically said that you never hear the wind in itself, only the storm whistling in the chimney, the wind in the trees.[126] The same is true of the mesh itself. You never perceive it directly. But you can detect it in the snails, the sea thrift, and the smell of the garbage can. The mesh is known through the being of the strange stranger.

The ecological thought understands that there never was an authentic world. This doesn't mean that we can do what we like with where we live, however. Thinking big means realizing that there is always more than our point of view. There is indeed an environment, yet when we examine it, we find it is made of strange strangers. Our awareness of them isn't always euphoric or charming or benevolent. Environmental awareness might have something intrinsically uncanny about it, as if we were seeing something we shouldn't be seeing, as if we realized we were caught in something.

2
Dark Thoughts

Strangers passing in the street
By chance two separate glances meet
And I am you and what I see is me
And do I take you by the hand
And lead you through the land
And help you understand the best I can?

Pink Floyd

We shall now go further, down into the darkness. How deep? Is it deep? Will we know when we are near the bottom? The journey is disorienting. Perhaps we aren't going down at all. Perhaps we're going in. In a response to deep ecology, I once called this "depthless ecology": either unimaginably deep or having no depth at all—we can never tell. In the end, I decided to call it *dark ecology*.[1]

It will be like going into the heart of the computer HAL 9000 in Stanley Kubrick's *2001: A Space Odyssey*. The astronaut Dave disarms HAL by dismantling its structure, piece by piece.[2] Dark ecology makes the world safe for the ecological thought. The only way out is down. It is the ultimate detox. But like homoeopathy, it uses poison as medicine. Rather than closing our ears and making loud noises to combat the sound of anti-ecological words, we shall absorb them and neutralize them from within.

Knowing more about interconnectedness results in more uncertainty. Staying with uncertainty is difficult; plenty of environmental ideology shirks it. We discovered the strange stranger, the unexpected arrival, the being about whom we know less than we presume. Is the strange stranger the same as us or different? Is the strange stranger alive? How can we tell? Is the strange stranger a person? What is a person? Are we people?

Art's ambiguous, vague qualities will help us think things that remain difficult to put into words. Reading poetry won't save the planet. Sound science and progressive social policies will do that. But art can allow us to glimpse beings that exist beyond or between our normal categories.

MUTATION, MUTATION, MUTATION

The Origin of Species begins with an extraordinary image of existence as coexistence:

> [Mistletoe] draws in nourishment from certain trees, which has seeds that must be transported by certain birds, and which has flowers with separate sexes absolutely requiring the agency of certain insects to bring pollen from one flower to the other. . . . [I]t is equally prepos- terous to account for the structure of this parasite, with its relations to several distinct organic beings, by the effects of external condi- tions, or habit, or the volition of the plant itself.[3]

There is no environment as such. It's all "distinct organic beings." Organ- isms can manipulate other organisms' muscles and senses.[4] Existence is coexistence or, as Darwin puts it, "adaptation." This doesn't mean what laissez-faire ideology wants it to mean: life is hard, and there it is, so get used to it or die, as if we were jigsaw pieces (only the ones that "fit" sur- vive). You can't get an "ought" from an "is" in any case: evolution doesn't tell you how to behave.[5] Darwin describes the misunderstood "struggle for existence":

> How have all those exquisite adaptations of one part of the organisa- tion to the other part, and to the conditions of life, and of one dis- tinct organic being to another being, been perfected? We see these beautiful co-adaptations most plainly in the woodpecker and mistletoe; and only a little less plainly in the humblest parasite which clings to

the hairs of a quadruped or feathers of a bird; in the structure of the beetle which dives through the water; in the plumed seed which is wafted by the gentlest breeze; in short, we see beautiful adaptations everywhere and in every part of the organic world.[6]

What a fine mesh we've gotten ourselves into. Wonderstruck, Darwin observes small, slight things clinging to hairs, slipping into water, and wafting on the breeze. Water and air are like hairs and feathers. Living and nonliving beings become the medium in which other beings exist. "Struggle for existence" doesn't necessarily translate into dog-eat-dog. It means the simple dependence of one being on another, like a desert plant depending on moisture.[7]

There is no static background. What we call Nature is monstrous and mutating, strangely strange all the way down and all the way through. Reading the Book of Nature is momentously difficult. Darwin's texts resemble other monumental nineteenth-century works, such as the first volume of Marx's *Capital* or the opening of Dickens's *Bleak House*. Piece by weird piece, one is let in on a vast, frighteningly complex world. Each text begins with a mysterious clue. Marx begins with a coat, Dickens begins with fog—Darwin begins with pigeon fanciers. The big picture creeps up on the reader like an atmosphere. The texts themselves model the gigantic, environmental, immersive phenomena they describe: the disturbing, Kafkaesque system of bureaucracy and law (Dickens), the phantasmagorical world of capital (Marx), and the illegible text once called the Book of Nature (Darwin).

The Book of Nature is more like a Mallarmé poem than a linear, syntactically well organized, unified work. The words spread out on the page: we can't tell whether to read from left to right, nor can we tell which words go with which. The words fluctuate and change position before our eyes.[8] Darwin himself uses the analogy. The history of life forms is like a book. Many pages are lacking: we can infer them only from the few remaining ones. (Not every living being existed in a place that the sea overwhelmed so as to fossilize it.)[9] Within those pages, whole paragraphs are missing or fragmented: "I look at the natural geological record, as a history of the world imperfectly kept, and written in a changing dialect."[10] Within existing paragraphs, there are incomplete sentences. (Successful species, for example, tend to make their immediate "family" extinct, so it's difficult to trace their history.)[11] Within existing sentences, some words seem to lack a letter or two. And some letters might not be letters at all, just squiggles. Interpreting the book depends upon interpreting the blanks between the marks, letters, words, sentences, paragraphs, and pages. Is there something in the blanks, or nothing? How can we tell? Derrida, eat your heart out.[12] Contrary to what some humanists think, it is not big news to Darwinism that "species" don't really exist.[13] What a work of repression we have wrought. Darwin shares with Freud and Marx the honor of having his theory declared dead every few weeks, as if it were necessary to kill the corpse over and over again.[14]

It gets worse. Consider a dialect, a local version of a particular language. No one can point to a specific person who spoke its first words.[15] Now consider chimpanzees. When chimps evolved, no observer could have said, "Hey! Look at that ape over there! That looks like a new species. Let's call it a chimp." Only later can someone do that. No one stood around in some thirteenth-century street, furtively chatting with a cadre of co-conspirators: "I know, let's really shake things up. Let's have the Renaissance. We'll invent perspective and travel round Africa using maps derived from this technology, find the Spice Islands, and form city-states and joint stock companies. Oh, and let's figure out a new, more individualistic version of Christianity and prove that the Earth goes round the Sun." No: several hundred years later, we look back at that moment and call it the Renaissance. Causality works backward. You can name something only retroactively. Something identical happens in evolution. When you look at a "species," you are looking at the past. When we look at organs, we're looking at a text—a record of past variations and adaptations.[16] We can't specify species rigorously without succumbing to what Dawkins calls "the tyranny of the discontinuous mind."[17] Only dead (extinct) intermediaries suggest sharp-seeming boundaries between species.[18] Yet continuity is as much of an illusion as is discontinuity.[19] Anti-essentialism is also dogmatic. The effects of the discontinuous mind are not trivial. Denying that humans are continuous with nonhumans has had disastrous effects. Yet declaring that humans are "animals" risks evening out all beings the better to treat them as instruments. Humans may be "animals," but "animals" aren't "animals."

The retroactivity of naming a species is like reading a poem. The words are already there, in a weird "will-have-been read" state (the future anterior). Darwin discusses "Artificial Selection" (breeding) as follows:

A man preserves and breeds from an individual with some slight deviation of structure . . . and the improved individuals slowly spread in the immediate neighbourhood. But as yet they will hardly have a distinct name, and from being only slightly valued, their history will be disregarded. When further improved by the same slow and gradual process, they will spread more widely, and will get recognised as something distinct and valuable, and will then probably receive a first provincial name. . . . But the chance will be infinitely small of any record having been preserved of such slow, varying, and insensible changes.[20]

Events of awareness, recognition, and naming retroactively posit the existence of new creatures, cutting into the smooth continuum of slight changes. There are no rivers as such, only river stages.[21] Recognizing and naming species and varieties is like putting a stick in a river and saying, "This is river stage *x*." For example, consciousness, which evolved piecemeal over millions of years, is nothing like the Boeing 747 to which the astronomer Fred Hoyle compared the evolution of simple cells. Nor is consciousness like the designer of the plane. A whirlwind assembling a Boeing 747 in a junkyard would indeed raise eyebrows. But the plane components are already plane components. Because causality works backward, we needn't worry about "intelligent design." Backward causality means that there is no intentionality whatsoever. The intentionality gets stuck onto evolving life forms later.

Things get weirder. Forget naming the chimps, and just concentrate on an ape growing some features that look chimplike. At no point can you say, "Hey, look at that proto-chimp." You might just be able to do so, says Darwin, but only with great difficulty and only after becoming an expert reader of life forms. And "expert" means that you have had to drop your rigid ideas about species.[22] So how keen will you be to name this being a proto-chimp? Imagine that the next stage of chimphood is a variant called a *chomp*. When will you be able to say, "That's not a chimp, that's a chomp-to-be"? (There is a correct answer.) Now imagine chomps evolving into a whole new species called a *champ*. How will you be able to distinguish between the highly developed chomp and the champ-as-such? Things get weirder still, because the retroactive effect is hardwired into evolution. For a mutation to count, it must be passed on. A single mutation is not an event. For something to happen, it must happen at least twice.[23]

Darwin identifies three kinds of development: species, variants, and monsters.[24] All three are hopelessly compromised and confused. When you look at two very similar organisms, are you looking at one species or more than one? Let's say you decide you're looking at just one: you must then decide, are you looking at a species and its variant? Which one is the species, and which is the variant? (Different biologists will give different answers, and the problem was compounded in Darwin's day by the lack of DNA evidence.)[25] As Darwin puts it, "species of all kinds are only well-marked and permanent varieties."[26] We may dispense with the idea of "permanence," since evolution itself depends upon impermanence. Then there is the idea of a species being "well-marked." This is a matter of degree, which is why Darwin uses the word "well." Some marks are more different than others. Suppose you decide you're looking at variants. Fair enough. Are you sure? Are the enlarged ears of chomps an example of monstrosity or an actual variation? Variation contaminates the idea of speciation, and monstrosity contaminates the idea of variation. All "adaptations" are at some previous point "exaptations"—uses of features for some novel, unintended purpose.[27] As Dawkins memorably declares, "We [humans] are modified worms swimming on our backs."[28] Insects and mammal bodies have a deep inner similarity: both possess Hox genes that code for segmentation.[29] All the way down, it's mutation, mutation, mutation.

The text of the organism is neither beautiful nor useful in any unified, lasting sense: "Nothing can be more hopeless than to attempt to explain [the] similarity in pattern in members of the same class, by utility or by the doctrine of final causes."[30] Organisms are palimpsests of additions, deletions, and rewritings, held together mostly by inertia.[31] Although moles, horses, porpoises, bats, and humans share similar-looking limbs, some strange protoplasm did not strive toward hands, wings, legs, flippers, and fins.[32] What about heterochrony—organs developing at non-normal times?[33] What about rudimentary limbs, such as male nipples?[34] If we keep thinking this way, Gnosticism might sound tempting: Creation exhibits the horrible accidents of a bungling god. Yet not even God is to blame: "Can we suppose that the formation of rudimentary teeth, which are subsequently absorbed, can be of any service to the rapidly growing embryonic calf by the excretion of precious phosphate of lime? When a man's fingers have been amputated, imperfect nails sometimes appear on the stumps."[35] Abstract infinity would be easier than this.

Marx, Freud, and Darwin describe processes taking place behind our backs. We can't see evolution, or the secret of the commodity form, or the unconscious. What Freud says about the unconscious is exactly what Darwin says about the evolving organism. The metaphor is writing. For Freud, the unconscious is like a "mystic writing pad," a children's toy that can be written on and erased: when you lift up the paper, you see a waxy surface, on which is inscribed everything ever written on the pad.[36] Life forms consist of layer upon archaeological layer of information. Behavior is also a picture of the past: habits that once had some function tend to persist, as Darwin notes in his fascinating exploration of the nonhuman origins of human expressions.[37] In their relative isolation, some ecosystems are records of prior times—think of Australian marsupials and monotremes such as the duck-billed platypus.[38]

Evolution jumbles bodies like a dream jumbles words and images. There is no negation in the unconscious and none in evolution. Things don't disappear; they become vestigial or mutate. Swim bladders in fish evolved into lungs in land animals.[39] They were not the "cause" of lungs, nor are they somehow analogous to them. In the language of literary analysis, swim bladders are not metaphorical or even metonymical. Metonymy means describing something by its causes or effects—a cigarette becomes a "smoke." How can a lung be a metonymy for a swim bladder? They are related yet unrelated—in no sense does a swim bladder "mean" or even "imply" lungs. Perfection is not on the menu: "If we admire the several ingenious contrivances, by which the flowers of the orchis and of many other plants are fertilised through insect agency, can we consider as equally perfect the elaboration by our fir-trees of dense clouds of pollen, in order that a few granules may be wafted by a chance breeze on to the ovules?"[40] Bees die when they sting, which is hardly pragmatic.[41]

Even monstrosity is problematic. A monster is something *seen* by someone (from the Latin *monstrare*, meaning to show).[42] Monstrosity is in the eye of the beholder. If there is anything monstrous in evolution, it's the uncertainty in the system at any and every point.[43] Amazingly, the contamination of variation, speciation, and so on is the reason why evolution works at all. Contamination is functional.[44] Darwin's world is about coexistence but not about harmony. It's like language. For meaning to happen, language must be noisy, messy, fuzzy, grainy, vague, and slippery. Evolution consists of incremental quantitative changes, not qualitative ones.[45] Biodiversity is good, because it means lots of fuzziness.[46] Darwin's Earth, then, manifests variety and continuity, but not some harmony of the one in the many, or of harmony in discord (*concordia discors*).[47]

All organisms are monsters insofar as they are *chimeras*, made from pieces of other creatures.[48] The strange stranger is strange to herself, or himself, or itself. Organs that evolved for one purpose can serve another. Living beings are not adapted to their environments, if by "adapted" we mean something like the idea of a round peg fitting a round hole. As we found in Chapter 1, a vulture's head, "beautifully adapted" (as described on television) for poking into piles of filth, was probably not bald for that reason. Young turkeys don't go sticking their heads into piles of filth.[49] There is no Natural hierarchy to which we should submit.

Mutant beings could be "so linked to [the species] by intermediate gradations" that no naturalist would feel comfortable classifying them as separate species.[50] But throwing in the towel and saying, "Oh well, there's nothing there" isn't a valid response either. We can't say for sure that there are specific entities out there. Yet you can surely tell the difference between a hawk and a daffodil. Now add the variable of gaps in the historical record. Say you didn't know what the "intermediate links" actually were, in a specific case. You would have to infer them by analogy—either they exist now but "somewhere else," or they existed "formerly." "And here," says Darwin, "a wide door for the entry of doubt and conjecture is opened."[51] It's like those doors in the De Chirico paintings in Chapter 1. They beckon sinisterly with present absence—or is it absent presence? Are the blanks in the Book of Nature absolute blankness or empty spaces where something used to be?

At the basis of "life" there is DNA, and it has no specific flavor. There is no chimp-flavored, no human-flavored DNA; we share 98 percent of our DNA with chimps and 35 percent with daffodils.[52] Some DNA is "junk

DNA," a free-riding, harmless parasite that doesn't get "expressed" in a phenotype at all.[53] At the DNA level, it becomes impossible to decide which sequence is "genuine" and which is a viral insertion: there is no DNA-flavored DNA. Moreover, there is no life-flavored DNA. Evolution theory deconstructs "life" itself. "Life" is a word for some self-replicating macro-molecules and their transport systems. But for "life" to start, there had to be a "pre-living life": otherwise, there would be an infinite regress or sudden creation from nothing. The movement that commences "life" is to be found *within* matter itself.[54]

"Life" may have arisen from RNA, the macromolecule that eventually became instrumental in translating DNA information to proteins. Sol Spiegelman's groundbreaking experiments solved the chicken-and-egg dilemma that DNA required ribosomes, which required DNA. In "RNA World," self-replicating molecules generated macromolecules like viruses, "parasites" without hosts.[55] For instance, consider viroids such as the Potato Spindle Tuber Viroid: these very ancient beings consist of a circle of RNA code. About ten times smaller than a virus, they probably began in RNA World. Nowadays they affect the transcription rather than translation parts of the host's reproductive machinery.

There's something slightly sizeist about viewing life as squishy, palpable substances, as if all life forms shared our kinds of tissue. This prejudice breaks down at high resolutions. Viruses are large crystals. The common cold virus is a short string of code packaged as a twenty-sided crystal; it tells DNA to make copies of itself. Is the rhinovirus "alive"? If you say yes, you ought to consider a computer virus alive. RNA-based beings such as viruses require hosts in order to replicate. Some of these macromolecules could have been swept up in the self-replication processes of a silicate. Ironically, silicon reproduction might predate organic (carbon-based) reproduction: "your great-great . . . grandmother *was* a robot!"[56] There is no life as such, however much we believe in slimy protoplasm. Viral code doesn't contain instructions for building an "organism." Instead, the code resembles a sentence that says something like, "There is a derivation of me in system x" (system x being a certain configuration of enzymes). Viruses are structurally incomplete. Like Coleridge's Life-in-Death, they are neither alive nor nonalive in a commonsensical way.[57]

At the University of California at Davis, Evolution 101 courses commence with a study of algorithms: repeated sets of mechanical calculations. All the way down to the sub-DNA level, evolution is a set of algorithmic processes. That's the disturbing thing about "animals"—at bottom they are vegetables. (Movie monsters such as zombies tend to resemble animated plants.) Our prejudice about vegetables is that they are beings that do only one thing—grow. The trouble with vegetable growth is that it consists of sets of algorithms—iterated functions, often producing fractal shapes like the Cantor set, tending toward infinity while resting in the palm of your hand. Consider *The Algorithmic Beauty of Plants*, a beautifully illustrated text readily available online.[58] Instead of illustrating plants, you can generate algorithms that would assemble them when you hit the Return key. Doesn't this mean that plants as such are an algorithmic process? This is why plant scientists now model plant growth using software like the authors developed. If you can write an algorithm that produces a rose by plotting a set of equations, surely the thing itself is a map of its genome, a three-dimensional expression of the algorithm's unfolding?

In the first chapter, we saw how time-lapse photography disturbs a Natural view of life forms. Furthermore, life forms are already time-lapse images. This is a strange and wonderful way to look at flowers. You could see daffodils as pictures of how an algorithm has manifested in "phase space," the space that plots all the states of the flower as a system. At the base of the daffodil, where it joins the stem, you see traces of how the flower looked when it started to spread upward and outward. You're looking at the daffodil's past, as well as at the past development of the flower as a species (as stated earlier). Think of the rings of a tree. Your face is a map of everything that happened to it. Thinking this way spookily undermines Nature from every angle and on every time scale. The ecological thought eats through the life–nonlife distinction. We can abandon all variations of Romantic vitalism—that is, believing in a vital spark separate from the material organization of life forms. Material organization turns out to be sets of formal relationships, not squishy stuff.

LET HE WHO IS WITHOUT "SIM"
CAST THE FIRST STONE

Evolution isn't all about competing for scarce resources. Brilliant colors and dramatic displays in insects, birds, and mammals have to do with sexual selection. Strange strangers evolve intricate and gorgeous ways of attracting a mate. For Alfred Russel Wallace, who developed a theory of evolution at the same time as Darwin, sexual selection seemed too arbitrary. He wanted "animal" displays to be a code for health.[59] The trouble is, one code is as good as another, so we risk an infinite regress if we don't accept some degree of nonutilitarian gorgeousness in sexual selection. Why choose an iridescent tail if one with purple spots would "cost" as much to produce? Healthiness is in the eye of the beholder, after all.

Darwin's enumeration of sexual display is almost comically vast. It builds toward his conclusion that racial difference has nothing to do with climate adaptation or "fitness," but instead with sheer aesthetic preference. Being quick and dirty, mutation is random with respect to current need, as we saw in Chapter 1. It would be very cumbersome for DNA code to carry a picture of the "environment" inside itself. Natural selection can't touch phenomena that are "neither useful nor injurious."[60] There is no reason for my skin color and reddish facial hair, except that someone thought it looked okay—at any rate, these features didn't put her off. As my daughter remarked, "Your bristles are completely useless. All they do is irritate me."

Let's just spell out what this means so that it's incredibly clear: there is no biological race as such. Biological race is a racist concept. When white supremacists talk about their "race" being threatened with "extinction," they are not describing reality. *The Descent of Man* undermines racist theories of skin color—for instance, those of Louis Agassiz, the biologist who promoted those unsettling racial terms such as "Caucasian." If there is no species as such, there can be no race as such.

Darwin records birds displaying their feathers in the following terms: they do so "to excite, attract, or fascinate the females"; their display is meant to "charm" and is "glittering," "superb, though to our eyes, grotesque," "splendid," and "beautiful"; the feathers have "beautiful ocelli [eye-like patterns]," and they are "remarkable," "wonderful objects," with the "most elegant patterns," "brilliantly coloured."[61] Concerning the ornamented wing feathers of the Argus pheasant, he writes, "these feathers are quite hidden on all ordinary occasions, but are fully displayed, together with the long secondary feathers, when they are all expanded together so as to form the great fan or shield."[62] Darwin continues:

> Many will declare that it is utterly incredible that a female bird should be able to appreciate fine shading and exquisite patterns. It is undoubtedly a marvellous fact that she should possess this almost human degree of taste. He who thinks that he can safely gauge the discrimination and taste of the lower animals may deny that the female Argus pheasant can appreciate such refined beauty; but he will then be compelled to admit that the extraordinary attitudes assumed by the male during the act of courtship, by which the wonderful beauty of his plumage is fully displayed, are purposeless.[63]

In other words, you're damned if you do, and you're damned if you don't.

Behavior and display go beyond sheer survival. Chimps paint and do rain dances. Perhaps nonhumans are capable of aesthetic contemplation, enjoying things for no reason. This possibility is far more profound than questions such as "Can animals feel things?" or "Can animals think?" It's a philosophical commonplace that nonhumans can't introspect, or self-reflect, so their suffering can't be taken as seriously as human suffering. Let's find out. Can nonhumans self-reflect? Some recent studies have answered "Yes," providing evidence based on states such as uncertainty and hesitation, which is good news for dark ecology.[64] Can humans self-reflect? Is self-reflection important when it comes to suffering? *The Descent of Man* is crystal clear: nonhumans can reason and imagine; they have a sense of beauty and wonder.[65] Darwin describes the mental contortions people go through to buttress disbelief in nonhuman cognition. A hundred and fifty years later, the latest cognitive science claims can still be found to have their roots in Darwin, and more besides: "birds appear to have nearly the same taste for the beautiful as we have. This is shewn by our enjoyment of the singing of birds, and by our women . . . decking their heads with borrowed plumes. . . . In man, however . . . the sense of beauty is manifestly a far more complex feeling, and is associated with various intellectual ideas."[66] By "far more," Darwin implies that differences between humans and nonhumans are matters not of quality, but of quantity, "of degree and not of kind."[67]

Do nonhumans possess language? Yes. How about imagination? Check. Reason? Copy that. A sense of mind? No doubt.[68] Can they use tools? Indeed. Do they display improved skills and learning over time? Absolutely. Can nonhumans feel compassion? Of course. Do they have a sense of humor? Why not? How about wonder? Yes. Choice? Also yes. Humans are fairly uniquely good at throwing and sweating: not much of a portfolio.[69] Read Darwin on female insects: "when we see many males pursuing the same female, we can hardly believe that the pairing is left to blind chance—that the female exerts no choice, and is not influenced by the gorgeous odours or other ornaments with which the male is decorated."[70] If butterflies have the capacity to make a choice, then surely it's game over for rigid distinctions between humans and nonhumans?

If it walks like a mind and quacks like a mind, why not call it one? The Turing Test for artificial intelligence (AI) suggests that subjectivity might be a performance.[71] The test pits a human against a nonhuman (say, some software), both hidden from view. If an interviewer can't distinguish between them in a reasonable time—if she can't figure out which one, if any, is the machine (or nonhuman)—then for all intents and purposes, the being is a person. Yet it would be more economical to say, employing our "less than" view, "Since I can't distinguish between your answers and what I think of as the answers of a person, you are someone I would have difficulty not characterizing as a person. In short, you are not a nonperson." Doesn't this mean that humans are strictly *not nonpersons?* Look at it the other way around. It's likely that AI will be a strange stranger: "we will have a very hard time deciding when and if we are dealing with an AI program, or just a 'weird' program."[72] Doesn't this mean that we already have a hard time distinguishing ourselves as "naturally" cognizant and not just "weird"? Instead of figuring out whether it's true to say, "Programs are as competent as us," we might be better off asserting, "We are as incompetent as programs." We could categorize life forms according to weakness and vulnerability, rather than strength and mastery, and thus build platforms for finding solidarity in our shared incompetence.

The general amazement that nonhumans possess "human" traits isn't surprising. A reader of Darwin's books—they aren't difficult and were sold at railway stations when they first appeared—can only conclude that a sustained effort of active ignorance and repression could have made stories about signing bonobo chimps as newsworthy as they are. As for the capitalist ideology that claims Darwin as its man—it's astounding given the staggering amount of evidence Darwin amasses to show that the ecosystem is not about blind, aggressive competition and six-pack ab-style "fitness."[73]

Perhaps aesthetic contemplation is a general trait, rather than a human, or *the* human, one. Even if it's restricted to a few life forms, should we deem it a "high" achievement or a default mental mode? Many philosophers dispute that nonhumans can contemplate. The supposedly exclusively human ability to contemplate is the cornerstone of Schopenhauer's bleak view of the Universe as a gigantic restaurant: we can escape only by denying our will to live, for which we find a model in artistic contemplation.[74] It's also the cornerstone of Neoplatonism: through art and philosophy, man rises from the brutish to the angelic. Environmentalism sometimes suggests that consciousness is a shameful anthropocentric crime. What if consciousness were not "higher" but "lower" than we have supposed?

Neuroscientists Francisco Varela, Evan Thompson, and Eleanor Rosch discuss training robots to the insect level; conversely, maybe humans could be trained to the mouse level.[75] Perhaps sentience isn't a "higher" function, but the most general (the "lowest") function. Some AI philosophers claim that machines can be self-aware.[76] Is even this necessary? Does consciousness have to be intentional? Does it have to be consciousness of some *x*, as both pro-AI and anti-AI philosophers suggest?[77] Perhaps consciousness is simply a recursive feature of the "on" state—less than self-consciousness, to be sure, yet providing a platform for it.[78] There is something like this in the idea of Buddha nature—in theory, a worm could become a Buddha, as a worm. The ecological thought should not set consciousness up as yet another defining trait of superiority over nonhumans. Our minds are hugely quantitatively different from other terrestrial minds but perhaps not qualitatively.[79]

Marx wrongly asserts that humans alone create their environment. Everyone is at it. *Atta*, the leaf-cutting ant, has towns of millions housing domesticated fungi that don't live anywhere else on Earth.[80] Corals live symbiotically with algae. Coral builds its own world, as do trees.[81] Why distinguish between conscious and unconscious behavior or, as Marx puts it, between "the worst architect and the best of bees"?[82] John Searle, an anti-AI philosopher, gets so excited about the idea that intelligence must be recognizable as such that he assumes we recognize it when it's wrapped in a specific package—say, a human skin.[83] Philosophers of consciousness either say, "We do not really know exactly what intentionality is, but we will" (these fall into the pro-AI camp), or, "We don't really know how bio-chemistry produces consciousness, but we will" (these fall into the anti-AI camp). Language about problems that have almost been solved switches on my ideology warning light. What if this unsolved status were a symptom of blindness to the lowly simplicity of consciousness? What if conscious-ness, like Nature, was one of those "less than" phenomena of the mesh?

We assume that consciousness is a special bonus prize for being more "highly evolved"—a suspicious idea from a Darwinist point of view. Per-haps being super isn't all it's cracked up to be. If we use science only to justify our superiority to other beings, the most we shall offer them is a condescending sympathetic hand. Yet as soon as we try to exit the model that puts humans at the top, we run into trouble. The ultimate philoso-pher of superiority was Friedrich Nietzsche. Nietzsche threw down a sig-nificant gauntlet: he reduced living to asserting mastery, and mastery to domination. What happens when you try to rise above his argument? You fall prey to his logic of mastery. Nietzsche's idea eats away at all positions that strive to overcome it. How do we get out of this trap? By crouching low and crawling away, like a sensible small mammal, or like Danny in *The Shining*.[84] We should think like losers, not winners.[85] Consciousness then becomes a property of lowliness and weakness, rather than of power. If an earthworm can be Buddha, then not all people are humans. Person-hood is strange strangeness.

Humans choose each other for meaningless, nonutilitarian, aesthetic reasons. Since Freud, we have grown used to associating art with sexual-ity. Darwin's theory of sexual selection brings these two spheres of life even closer: think of a peacock's tail. There is in evolution not just ran-dom mutation and sheer redundancy—the earflaps and the rudimentary and vestigial organs—but also pure semblance, the realm of the aesthetic, "seeming" without "meaning." Humans specify nonhumans as members of this realm, to make them seem improper. To parrot, to ape—the names themselves pertain to semblance. When Dave, my sister- and brother-in-law's parrot, laughs at a comedy on television, is he really laughing? Or is he just imitating the canned laughter he hears and playing it back, like a sample? So am I myself laughing at the comedy? Is there anything like a single independent mind behind my laughing? Can I tell? That's the trouble with pure semblance: "What constitutes pretense is that, in the end, you don't know whether it's pretense or not."[86] Canned laughter relieves us of the burden of a response: to this extent, our response is already semblance. Darwin tells of a parrot who had recorded the lost language of a human tribe.[87] Evolution itself is a text that organisms "play back" automatically. We can "read" swim bladders in the form of lungs. Darwin asserts that what is hidden in life forms is right there on the surface, which is why it is so hard to see: the nearness of descent is "hidden . . . by various degrees of modification."[88] Isn't evolution ridiculously obvious, asks Darwin, when you consider how humans breed horses and pigeons? Like Marx's commodity and Dickens's London, evolution is an open secret.

The worrying thing isn't that pure semblance is an illusion. At least then you would know that it truly is an illusion and that there was a non-illusory reality within or behind the illusion, even if you couldn't access it. You could still say the illusion was false. The trouble with pure semblance is that it's *like an illusion*. You can't tell whether it's an illusion or not. We've seen how living beings are chimeras, made of other creatures' parts. The other sense of "chimera" has to do with fiction: "an unreal creature of the imagination, a mere wild fancy; an unfounded conception."[89] Monstrousness and illusoriness go together.

Given all this, the only thing to do is to treat beings as people, even if they turn out not to be. This is how director Werner Herzog gets it wrong in his film about Timothy Treadwell's life, *Grizzly Man*.[90] Egged on by devotees of deep ecology, Treadwell made documentaries about grizzly bears in Alaska for schoolchildren, only to eventually be eaten by the bears. Treadwell treated bears as if they were cuddly humans. Herzog's devastating documentary reveals the horrifying consequences of disappearing into one's Nature fantasy, which for Treadwell appeared both as an escape from something all too human and as the ultimate stage performance. Treadwell closed the gap between humans and bears. But

Herzog seems only too ready to keep it wide open. At least Treadwell was consistent. The bears who ate Treadwell weren't the ones whom he knew in his Alaskan sojourns—might this not prove Treadwell's point or at least weaken Herzog's? A fate worse than being eaten by wild bears in Alaska could well be Herzog making a documentary about you. Herzog's view of animal indifference and cruelty is as mistaken as Treadwell's view of animal sympathy. We're supposed to judge Treadwell from the cold distance of Herzog's bleak existential gaze—to regard Treadwell like hungry bears.

Herzog's bleakness, ironically, is far closer to wilderness-speak than Treadwell's cuddliness. Don't we have, in this pairing—cuddly closeness and the cold, sadistic gaze—the coordinates of conventional fantasies about strange strangers? Lewis Carroll was right in "The Walrus and the Carpenter" to show how pity for the living world is an aspect of a sadistic relish for devouring it: the Walrus weeps for the oysters as he pours them down his greedy throat.

In *The Wild Parrots of Telegraph Hill*, Mark Bittner, a Beat-ish, easygoing fellow who house-sits for the wealthy, decides to feed the parrots who congregate in San Francisco, not out of any deep sense of their identity, but just because he likes them.[91] Did the parrots fly there from somewhere else, or did they escape from cages in the city? No one is sure. I've heard environmentalists saying that Bittner should never have fed the parrots, as they weren't "natural" (that is, native). What happened to the huddled masses, yearning to be free? Shouldn't this ultimately apply to all strange strangers? Are we not all migrants? Don't we have an infinite responsibility for the neighbor? Bittner himself is a kind of parrot. The ecological thought thinks neither cuddliness nor wildness but uncanny familiarity. Remember John Clare's mouse, her "young ones hanging at her teats" ("Mouse's Nest," line 6): vulnerable, squirming life, experienced with honest wonder; a disturbed concern that undercuts rubbernecking fascination.

The deep green objection is that the parrots aren't really animals and that the film's view is anthropocentric. Here that we run into one of the greatest obstacles to the ecological thought, the sign saying, "No anthropocentrism." It's a dead end. The danger in political and philosophical thinking is to reckon that we have seen beyond ideology, that we can stand outside, say, "humanist" reality. This idea is itself humanism. Anthropocentrism assumes an "anthro" that is "centric." The problem resides not so much in the content as it does in the attitude that comes bundled with the accusation. The idea of anthropocentrism is that the "human" occupies a privileged nonplace, simultaneously within and outside the mesh. One accuses others of anthropocentrism from that place.

Everything we think becomes suspect, as we assume that there is a Nature from which our thinking can deviate. And deviancy must be punished. The position of hunting for anthropocentrism *is anthropocentrism*. To claim that someone's distinction of animals and humans is anthropocentric, because she privileges reason over passion, is to deny reason to nonhumans. We can't in good faith cancel the difference between humans and nonhumans. Nor can we preserve it. Doing both at the same time would be inconsistent. We're in a bind. But don't despair: kings felt less for peasants than they did for pheasants. The bind is a sign of an emerging democracy of life forms.

Putting strange strangers in a box damages them. One box is the "anything-but-human" one—the Gaia box, the "web of life" box, or the "more-than-human world" box. Another is the "all sentient beings are really just like humans" box. Another, newer, subtler box is the "sentient beings are neither human nor nonhuman" box. If there is no true self, then perhaps *there is a nonself.* There are many terms for this in contemporary philosophy, such as *assemblage, cyborg, postidentity,* or *posthumanity.* Likewise, if there is no Nature, perhaps *there is a non-Nature,* a world of interlocking machines, or a world where all was one and therefore God—pantheism, or philosopher Arne Naess's deep ecological version.

Naess claims, "identification [with the natural world can be] so deep that one's own self is no longer adequately delimited by the personal ego or organism. One experiences oneself to be a genuine part of all life."[92] The "ego or organism," doesn't delimit "One," but one can mysteriously still "experience oneself." Thus *there is a nonself.* Ideas like this merely "upgrade" the self. (To detect this, try substituting "England" or "Englishness" for "the natural world" and "life.") Ideas that *there is a nonself* and that *there is a non-Nature* domesticate the strange stranger. A true reductionist would stick with the idea that there is no self, not that there is a nonself. And isn't the self a paradox in any case? The phrase "I am me" shows how slippery the so-called self is, in "itself." There is no guarantee that the me who is telling you that I am me is the same as the me about whom I'm saying, "I am me."

Remember the Menger sponge, the fractal cube infinitely filled with infinitesimal holes: "an infinitely porous, spongy or cavernous texture without emptiness, caverns endlessly contained in other caverns."[93] The mesh isn't really a sponge—you can't wash your back with it. And the strange stranger is not a spongy self—you can't squeeze it. Menger sponges are good for thinking with—just don't expect to see one "over yonder" any time soon. They are infinite. Consider the ancestor of the Menger sponge, the Cantor set. There are infinitely many points in the Cantor set; likewise, it contains infinitely many no-points. There is not something there; there is not nothing there. The ecological thought is not an unthinkable mystery—that would result in theism or nihilism. The ecological thought opens onto "un-thinking." Yet this doesn't mean that we should stop. It means that "thought" and "beyond thought" are not as opposed as we might think. It doesn't hurt that life forms tend to express DNA in fractal geometries that approach infinity. DNA plots branches, blood vessels, heartbeats, and forests like this.

Infinity implies intimacy: "To see a world in a grain of sand . . . Hold infinity in the palm of your hand" (Blake, *Auguries of Innocence*, lines 1–3).[94] Immediately following this cry of the heart, Blake's poem flips between animal cruelty and social misery. That's the paradox of the ecological thought: "A dog starv'd at his master's gate / Predicts the ruin of the state" (lines 9–10). Blake shows us infinity on *this* side of reality, not "over yonder" in some abstract ideal realm. The ecological thought concerns itself with personhood, for want of a better word. Up close, the ecological thought has to do with warmth and tenderness; hospitality, wonder, and love; vulnerability and responsibility. Although the ecological thought is a form of reductionism, it must be personal, since it refrains from adopting a clinical, intellectual, or aesthetic (sadistic) distance. Believing in an ineffable Nature or Self is wrong. But so is claiming that there is a thrilling, infinitely plastic post-Thing out there waiting to be completely manipulated. Both the Nature people and the post-Nature people have it in for, well, people. The ecological thought is about people—it is people.

Coexistence means nothing if it means only the proximity of other machines or sharing components with other machines. Upgraded models of "post-Nature" deprive us of intimacy. The ecological thought must think something like Georg Hegel's idea of the "night" of subjectivity, the "interior of nature." At the bottomless bottom, subjectivity is an infinite void.[95] When I encounter the strange stranger, I gaze into depths of space, far more vast and profound than physical space that can be measured with instruments. The disturbing depth of another person is a radical consequence of inner freedom. It's a mistake to think that the mesh is "bigger than us." Everything is intimate with everything else. The ecological thought is vast, but strange strangers are right next to us. They are us. Inner space is right here, "nearer than breathing, closer than hands and feet."[96] Rather than a vision of inclusion, we need a vision of intimacy. We need thresholds, not spheres or concentric circles, for imagining where the strange stranger hangs out.

If the mesh were really a "thing" separate from its interconnected members, then we would be out of trouble, because there would be something "over yonder" we could admire from a distance. All we have to go on are unique manifestations. How can we know what's what? The trouble with pure appearance is that we can't reduce it to straightforward truth. How can I ever really know that there isn't a key in your neck or that I'm not a robot? Can I ever successfully tell the sentient sheep from the android goats?

At the fairground in Steven Spielberg's movie *AI: Artificial Intelligence*, humans line up at a circus to destroy androids, in what they suppose is a harmless exercise of sadism on mere machines. The ringmaster Lord Johnson-Johnson shouts, "Let he who is without 'sim' cast the first stone."[97] He means that humans have a right to destroy machines, but in quoting Jesus, the circus master disturbs us. "Sim" (simulation, semblance) resembles "sin." Humans think that they are natural, that is, without sin/sim. Yet if they truly considered the androids as mere machines, wouldn't it be unsatisfying to destroy them? Surely the sadistic fun comes from at least imagining that they are sentient? Jesus means that none of us are without sin. By extension, none of us are without sim.

Precisely because we can't tell whether the AI beings are alive and sentient, we should deem ourselves responsible for them. To project our wishes onto them is to betray them, for then they become representations of racist fantasies (a minstrel robot is shot out of a canon). The same principle

applies in *Blade Runner*. Since we can't tell whether the replicants are humans (or whether we are replicants, or whether humanness itself consists
of replicant-ness), we're responsible for them.

Consider the inverse fact: intense experiences often seem not to be happening to "us." They redefine who "we" are. Which came first, the psychological symptom or the subject "of" that symptom? Wordsworth grap-
ples with this in his long poems. As a point of comparison, consider a scene
in *Star Trek: First Contact*, in which a cyborg "Borg" queen grafts a piece of
skin onto Data, the android, to introduce him to a world of sensations.[98] It
is as if the zero level of identity is sheer sensation. But wait a minute—why
does Data gasp with pleasure, or pain, or both, when the queen blows on
the skin, the hairs wafting gently under her breath like seaweed? Doesn't
this imply that he already has a psyche? Inner space seems to have existed
before it was filled with "objects" such as sensations. Traumas become
traumas only after the fact. It is like Einstein's view of matter as the curvature of space: in essence, the psyche is this minimal distortion. Both the
surface and the depth of our being are ambiguous and illusory. In his auto-
biographical poem *The Prelude*, when Wordsworth tells how his former
self had powerful experiences (the "spots of time"), there are descriptions
of the experience being missed, or less than expected, or blank.[99] Wordsworth improved on most eagerly affirmative Nature writers before they
were even born. It is far more faithful to say, "The experience was so intense, I wasn't even sure I was having it, or whether there was a me to have
it at all. For days afterward, I just felt empty and weird."

We can't be sure whether sentient beings are machines or not. And it
would be dangerous if we thought we could. Inner depth might just be an
illusion. And still weirder, this illusion might have actual effects. My uncertainty about this, evoking the uncanny, is essential to the encounter
with the strange stranger. However much we try, we can't explain the
strange stranger away. We're stuck with the paradoxes of pure appearance. We have to care for a world that presents itself in an illusion-like
way that we can't ignore. Loving the strange stranger has an excessive,
unquantifiable, nonlinear, "queer" quality. There is something utterly outrageous and, at the same time, universal and unavoidable about it, something the phrase "tree hugger" fails to capture. In a perfect inversion of
Herzog's relationship with Treadwell, the director of *The Wild Parrots of*

Telegraph Hill falls in love with Mark Bittner. Bittner's love for the parrots and Treadwell's love of the bears transcend habitual affection for other sentient beings. Yet all affection has an exorbitant quality. Out of the universe of things, I choose you. This is another reason why the aesthetic of cuteness won't fly for all sentient beings, all at once.

Texts are messages in bottles. The reader is the future of the text. The text addresses a strange stranger, beyond and above the specific addressees of the specific message. Are you an android, you who are reading this? Are you a person? Are you reading this three thousand years from now in some impossible-for-me-to-imagine future, in some impossible-for-me-to-imagine form? Does my awareness of your awareness of my awareness of your future being affect this writing?

The text contains a void into which the reading mind leaps.[100] Meaning depends on unmeaning. Evolution is a text like this. Just like reading a novel loaded with "too much" information, the more details we find, the more gaps we perceive.[101] The more we know about strange strangers, the more we sense the void. Determined to think interconnectedness to the end, the ecological thought produces a mental openness far more disturbing than outer space. The openness exists on the intimate level of the encounter with the strange stranger. I mean this differently than Jean-Paul Sartre, who in an allergic way finds the existence of others to be a "drain hole" in one's being. Other minds are like the dark side of the Moon: there, but invisible to us.[102] Our intimacy is an allowing of and a coming to terms with the passivity and void of the strange stranger. And since the strange stranger is us, the void is us, too. This is very good news. We have a platform for compassion rather than condescending pity, and therefore, we have a basis for reimagining democracy. The inbuilt uncanniness of strange strangers is part of how we can be intimate with them.

Democracy implies coexistence; coexistence implies encounters between strange strangers. Are there any ways of modeling this encounter? If we're not casting stones, since we're not without sim/sin, what are we doing instead? Democracy is based on reciprocity—mutual recognition. But since, at bottom, there is no way of knowing for sure—since the strange stranger aspect of personhood confronts me with a terrifying darkness— the encounter at its zero level is a pure, absolute openness and is thus asymmetrical, not equal. The stranger is infinity.[103] Since the strange stranger is not my mirror, there is no way of knowing whether she, or he, or it is a person. So before we get to mutual recognition, we must have radical openness. There are many difficulties here.[104] The encounter is loving, risky, perverse. Because the strange stranger is uncanny and uncertain, she, he, or it gives us pause. The fact that the strange stranger might bite is the least of our worries. It is more like how feminist Luce Irigaray puts it, when she imagines the nonhuman as a teacher and the nonhuman–human relationship as a model for future ways of human being.[105]

Sentient beings do suffer—that is practically the definition of sentience. Some assert that suffering distinguishes life forms from artificial intelligence. What about bacteria? Where is the limit below which a being can't be considered to be sentient? Wouldn't this possibly include some AI, and therefore, at least in theory, couldn't AI suffer? If you're prepared to claim that thinking is "emergent" like a cloud or a stock market pattern, shouldn't you be prepared to say that consciousness can exist without a specific skin in which to wrap it?[106]

QUEER DUCKS

These questions extend Turing's proposition that if a machine walks like a mind and quacks like a mind, it might as well be one.[107] The uncanny and uncertainty are basic to the ecological thought. If we try to get rid of them, we conjure up Nature that rises up to judge, monitor, and discipline: we don't love Nature properly; we should act natural; unnaturalness will be noted and punished. Environmentalism has been trapped in ideologies of masculinity, the ultimate performance of nonperformance, the ultimate imitation of Nature. This goes not only for subjects who experience Nature but also for objects—Nature itself. We often think of Nature as female. But Nature is also masculine, if masculinity means a desperate attempt to peel the feminine dimension of pure semblance away from one's being.

Rugged, bleak, masculine Nature defines itself through extreme contrasts. It's outdoorsy, not "shut in." It's extraverted, not introverted. It's heterosexual, not homosexual. It's able-bodied—"disability" is nowhere to be seen, and physical "wholeness" and "coordination" are valued over the spontaneous body.[108] As the private school motto put it, "a sound mind in a sound body." Nature is aggressively healthy, hostile to self-absorption. It's allergic to semblance. Appearance should have a point: those mountains over there must be about themselves, or my soul, or Nature, and so on. There is no room for irony, no room for anything more than superficial ambiguity. Things should mean what they say and say what they mean. There is no room for humor, except perhaps a phobic, "hearty" kind. Masculine Nature is the operating system of the authoritarian personality.

Masculine Nature fears its own shadow—subjectivity itself. It wants no truck with the night of the world, the threateningly empty dimension of open subjectivity.[109] This dimension is feminine. "Feminine" is a term, perhaps a patriarchal one, for the open, purely apparent dimension of subjectivity.[110] Environmental phenomena exhibit this concrete infinity.[111] Levinas talks of the "defenseless eyes" of the face.[112] Masculine Nature is afraid of the nothingness of feminine "mere" appearance. It's the Trickster quality found in many indigenous cultures. When we approach the idea that all sentient beings are equal and free, we discover the Trickster.

The ecological thought gets along just fine with the Trickster. Thinking itself is tricky. When you think, you move from one place to another, from A to not-A. Like a magic show, thinking is this tricky play. The ecological thought is the Trickster, thinking of the Trickster. Turing's own wonderful example of his test is not about a human and a nonhuman but a man and a woman. The man has to convince the interviewer that he might be a woman, and vice versa. Is not this the height of Tricksterishness? And doesn't it demonstrate that identity is a performance— you can walk and quack like a duck, like a woman, like a mind?[113] This is about what evolutionists call "satisficing": instead of becoming optimal for their environments, living beings do just enough to look and quack like themselves.[114] The ecological thought might invert the conventional wisdom on virtual reality art, such as transgender artist Micha Cardinas's simulations of nonhuman existence, as a dragon in the online domain Second Life.[115] It's not that these simulations demonstrate posthuman platitudes about malleable identity (Cardinas's own estimation), but rather that identity as such is already a simulation—a performative display. Might this not imply that virtuality is hardwired into living substance? It's not just that rabbits are rabbits in name only: it's that whether or not we have words for them, rabbits are deconstructive all the way down—display happens at every level. Nothing is self-identical. We're embodied, yet without essence. True materialism would be nonsubstantialist: it would think matter as self-assembling sets of interrelationships in which information is directly inscribed: DNA is both matter and information.

The Trickster teaches us that subjectivity is an inescapable part of reality. Even if we are alone in the "wilderness," we are not alone. Our examination of the uncanny should demonstrate this. What is scary about being lost in a forest of tree upon tree, or lost in a city of street upon street, is catching a glimpse of yourself, from the point of view of the trees. It is the feeling of being watched, of being accompanied. And what are you seeing? What is seeing you? We can identify only a shadowy darkness. The dark openness gazes at us. We aren't exactly seeing ourselves in a mirror. We're seeing ourselves as the void that looks back at us, as if we looked in the mirror and saw a hooded figure, and underneath the hood was nothing. The uncanny path in the forest and the city goes round and round in circles.

The novel and movie *Into the Wild* (by Jon Krakauer and Sean Penn, respectively) reckon the terrible damage the masculine Nature meme can cause.[116] Christopher McCandless changes his name to Alexander Supertramp, evoking a gay Greek imperialist and disco lyricism—strange given his fatal experimentation with rugged male individualism. He only realizes that other people are important just before he dies from eating a poisonous plant, on his abandoned school bus home in the heart of Alaska. The "into the wild" fantasy is a syndrome, a social performance. In January 2008, Rice University student Matt Wilson disappeared into the wilderness with a fistful of money and a beard. Do these suicidal young men think they are disappearing into Nature? Supertramp was just a few miles from shelter and about fifteen miles from a major highway. His concept of wildness overrode his life instinct.

This is no journey into the wild but into the mind. Men (mostly men) like Supertramp think that they're escaping civilization and its discontents, but in fact they occupy the place of its death instincts. Their fantasy is of a world of absolute control and order: "I can make it on my own" is what American boys are taught to think. The "return to Nature" desperately acts out the myth of the self-made man, editing out love, warmth, vulnerability, and ambiguity. Even the aesthetic of the cute is a beginning of affection, so it's better than nothing. Warmth and vulnerability might not be served well by high art. What the ecological thought is thinking is unbeautiful, uncold, unsplendid.[117]

Masculine Nature is unrealistic. In the mesh, sexuality is all over the map. Our cells reproduce asexually, like their single-celled ancestors or the blastocyst that attaches to the uterus wall at the beginning of pregnancy. Plants and animals are hermaphrodites before they are bisexual and bisexual before they are heterosexual. Most plants and half of animals are either sequentially or simultaneously hermaphroditic; many live with constant transgender switching.[118] A statistically significant proportion of white-tailed deer (10 percent plus) are intersex.[119] Hermaphroditic snails curl around each other with seemingly palpable affection.[120] Seeking an encounter with another individual is good for plants, but they do it via other species such as insects and birds; thus bees and flowers evolve together, through mutually beneficial "deviations."[121] Heterosexual reproduction is a late addition to a gigantic ocean of asexual division.[122] And it looks like a good option (rather than a very expensive add-on) only from the "point of view" of macromolecular replicators.[123] It doesn't make sense from the standpoint of these molecules' vehicles (you and me and the beetles).

Try a simple experiment: can you see gay humans where you live? Good. Why do you think, after several hundred million years of homosexual behaviors, that gay life forms persist? Could it be that homosexuality is no problem, from DNA's point of view? Given that binary gender performance floats in a colossal welter of transgender, homosexual, and asexual phenotypes, isn't it time to drop the idea of Nature as a straight, binary, exclusive realm?

For about two hundred years, the heavy lifting for homophobic Nature has been organicism, which we've explored in its roles as a bearer of ideas of holism and squishiness. Organicism polices the sprawling, tangled, queer mesh by naturalizing sexual difference. Biologist Joan Roughgarden argues that gender diversity is a necessary feature of evolution. Moreover, her argument is possible because Darwin himself opened a space for it. Strict Darwinism is profoundly anti-teleological (Marx liked it for this reason). Individuals and species don't abstractly "want" to survive to preserve their form: only macromolecular replicators "want" that. From the replicators' viewpoint, if it doesn't kill you ("satisficing"), you can keep it, whatever it is.[124] A vast profusion of gender and sex performances can arise. As far as evolution goes, they can stay that way. Thinking otherwise is "adaptationism."

The ecological thought is also friendly to disability. There are plentiful maladaptions and functionless phenomena at the organism level. Webbed feet may be "beautifully adapted to swimming"—but coots get along just fine without them. Functionality only really manifests at the genomic level. Why are there organisms at all, as a matter of fact? Only because it benefits some replicators to clump together.[125] As we saw, it's better to think of organs without bodies than of discreet, self-contained, and self-identical organisms. Sphex wasps paralyze crickets to feed to their young. If you move a paralyzed cricket from in front of the burrow that the Sphex wasp who paralyzed her is inspecting (for the presence of grubs), the wasp will repeat the same behavior, moving the cricket back meaninglessly to the entrance of the hole, without dragging her in.[126] Nature only looks natural because it keeps going, and going, and going, like the undead, and because we keep our distance, frame it, size it up. The mesh is made of prosthetic devices and algorithmic behaviors. An eye is a wet, squeezable pair of glasses. Legs are soft, brittle crutches. Ears are rather florid headphones. Brains are things that quack like minds.

Like a stream slipping around a large stone, the ecological thought flows past masculine Nature. The idea of species is far too rigid and arbitrary to account for the mutagenic, liquid strange stranger.[127] Every being is forked, bent, blind, deaf, mentally afflicted. Men have nipples because the common ancestor of humans and other apes was intersex.[128] Male nipples can secrete milk at puberty and birth, and it's likely that "during a former prolonged period male mammals assisted females in nursing their offspring."[129] Indeed, says Darwin, "at a very early embryonic period both sexes possess true male and female glands. Hence some remote progenitor of the whole vertebrate kingdom appears to have been hermaphrodite or androgynous."[130] If you ignore the nipples, males look almost male.

Welcome pine trees with their profuse clouds of pollen, welcome grandmothers with dogs, and boo to philosophers who should know better who disparage grandmothers with dogs in favor of wolves.[131] For such thinkers, if there can't be a return to Nature, there should be a return to non-Nature. Pets are queer animals, not Natural. They may be neutered, but they have many ways of expressing affection and sexuality. They form a bionic hybrid coexistence with their guardians.[132] The cute still has some juice left. Just because the cute is limited, we shouldn't exchange it for the "into the wild" meme. We must make choices at some stage, so I vote not to throw out the cute baby with the "Natural" bathwater. The sickly-sweet subjects of the cute are better for human and ecological survival than the deadly sublime of "naked," unqueer Nature. The sentimental is about feeling tenderness.[133] Soft toys induce love. The subtitle of *Wall•E* could be "cuteness saves the planet."[134] All that survives the mass evacuation of consumerists are ghostly sentimental fantasies. Criticize the cute, but not in the name of masculine Nature. In "sophisticated" discourse, sentimentality is something disgusting that other people have: "She is sentimental, you are too emotional, but I have genuine feelings." The perverse, dark side of the ecological thought wants to indulge this sentimentality a little. Anyway, there are no genuine (versus fake) emotions. They are all fake.

Okay, deep breath—it just isn't right to criticize genetic engineering as unnatural, as if decent people should ban horses, dogs and cats, wheat and barley. It isn't sound to call "technological" gene manipulation wrong, as if stud farming wasn't technical manipulation. Crossbreeding is a form of technology. Fields and ditches are technology. Apes with termite sticks are technological. And what is barley if not a queer plant? Biological beings are all queer. All food is Frankenfood.[135] The ecological thought might argue, provocatively I know, that genetic engineering is simply doing consciously what was once unconscious.[136] My DNA can be told to produce viruses—that's how viruses replicate. There isn't a little picture of me in my DNA: hence the swine flu, which evolved from viruses affecting three different species. Genomics can use a virus to tell bacterial DNA to make plastic rather than bacteria.

What's wrong about genetic engineering is that it turns life forms into private property to enrich huge corporations. Large, dynastic families controlled corporate capitalism all the way back to the spice race, the first space race.[137] Capitalism has always restricted gene pools and amassed large quantities of property, with accompanying stability and power. The capitalist language of deregulation, flow, and circulation masks the static, repetitive, "molar" quality of capitalist forms. But processes of privatization and ownership contradict the liquid, queer, mutagenic, shadowy, and ungraspable qualities of life forms. If we're going to resist genetically engineered life forms, we shall need to figure out why. Otherwise, our illusory reasons will produce in the long run just as illusory a result.

NEANDERTHALS "R" US

The strange stranger is not just the "other"—the "self" is this other. Since there is no (solid, lasting, independent, single) self, we are the strange stranger: "I is another."[138] Percy Shelley describes an encounter between a poet and an antelope in *Alastor:*

>   he would linger long
> In lonesome vales, making the wild his home,
> Until the doves and squirrels would partake
> From his innocuous hand his bloodless food,
> Lured by the gentle meaning of his looks,
> And the wild antelope, that starts whene'er
> The dry leaf rustles in the brake, suspend
> Her timid steps to gaze upon a form
> More graceful than her own.　　**(98–106)**[139]

The antelope seems capable of aesthetic contemplation, appreciation for no reason. Does she think, "This form is more graceful than my own"? We shall never know. Shelley doesn't say "a form / That she thought more graceful than her own." That's the beauty of narrative thoughts not tagged with an obvious "she thought" or "she remarked to herself that . . ." Not knowing opens up inner space, the space of the other mind. We glimpse the possibility that the nonhuman world is not impersonal. The police know that being startled is highly revealing of cognitive states.[140] Like Clare's wild duck, Shelley's antelope "suspending" her steps makes us wonder—could she be conscious like us?

Humans maintain the human–animal boundary by erecting rigid walls made of quasi-humans, humanoids, hominids, ambiguous nonhumans, or unhumans. The discovery of Neanderthals in 1848 opened up new areas for wall building.[141] Strangely, ideology (not science but scientism) craves a straight line from three-million-year-old Lucy the australopithecine through *Homo habilis* to humans, bypassing our near neighbors the Neanderthals.[142] Yet humans and Neanderthals share a common ancestor half a million years ago.

One brick in the wall is the idea that proper humans, unlike Neanderthals, possess an imagination, so they can think creatively about survival.[143] Yet recent research suggests that Neanderthal tools were at least as well made as human ones.[144] Neanderthal DNA contains the FOXP2 gene, suggestive of language use. The Neanderthals buried their dead with tools, in the fetal position, surrounded by horns, flowers, and herbs, and strewn with ochre.[145] You would have thought that this would have clinched it, but some still maintain that their burials were not elaborate enough to indicate imagination.

Or what we think of as "imagination" is just an after-image, an extrapolation we make when we notice people using language. Maybe an ant walking over the sand doesn't have a "picture" of the sand; maybe she just walks, as I did over the moraine glaciers of Mount Kailash.[146] I didn't have many ideas about moraine glaciers; I was just trying not to fall. We don't have to imagine intelligence as a way of picturing the world, as if each sentient being had to know Platonic solids before it could crawl.[147] Furthermore, do we have a sense of *world* in our heads, a background against which we can operate? Are certain discriminations really human—do they conform to some pre-given "world" of humanness? Perhaps the pre-givenness of the world is just a feature of its relatively slow rate of change, like the evolution of our bodies. If there were a Communist revolution, or if we suddenly grew an extra ear, things might seem different. Is education about conforming to a horizon at all? What if we ourselves were just following lists of instructions, plus awareness? What if our minds were just flipping back and forth from left to right brain activities, without a background or world?[148]

Anti-AI philosophers claim either that there are definite "things" that a mind thinks that are not reducible to other things; or that there is a definite world. The pro-AI view can't address the strangeness of the strange stranger. In each case, humans are too like nonhumans for comfort. Darwinism asserts that humans are "evolved apes," while pre-Darwinist thinking labeled apes "degenerate humans."[149] Linnaeus thought that orangutans should be classified as a species of *Homo*, and there is a movement afoot to reclassify bonobos this way—yet note in passing that there is no movement to reclassify humans as a species of *Pan* (chimpanzee), even though, technically, we are the third chimp, having more in common with them than gorillas do.[150]

There is a wonderful moment in the cartoon series *The Simpsons*, during the opening credits (whose final shot varies in each episode), where the original Simpsons meet their more recent incarnations.[151] Both families scream and run away from their doppelgängers. This captures precisely what is strange about the strange stranger, the implication of something that Darwin squirrels away in the first third of *The Descent of Man*: "In a series of forms graduating insensibly from some ape-like creature to man as he now exists, it would be impossible to fix on any definite point when the term 'man' ought to be used."[152] If transitions are smooth and incremental, we can't notice them. But by the same token, any successful variation tends to become less and less like its neighbors. The familiar becomes strange. The human–chimp boundary occurred as recently as six million years ago, which is last week from Earth's point of view.[153] Like many features of life forms, distinctive Neanderthal skulls evolved by chance.

Jean Auel's Neanderthals in *The Clan of the Cave Bear* are decidedly patriarchal, acting out scenes from a postwar America with an absurd combination of male sports and women's cook-offs. William Golding's world in *The Inheritors*, conversely, is matriarchal, and the different minds of the Neanderthals are deeply rendered in the descriptive layers of the narrative. Golding's Neanderthals are an endangered species, hunted and killed for sadistic sport by humans. It's not clear whether Lok and the others are Neanderthals.[154] By the time we find out, we have identified with them. Auel portrays the life of a human adopted into a Neanderthal clan. The clan finds it hard to accept a woman who is taller and smarter than anyone in their densely hierarchical and patriarchal structure. Despite being promoted to Medicine Woman, she is raped, beaten, and banished and separated from her son. The Neanderthals mirror contemporary human racism ("racism is Neanderthal"). This doesn't really abolish the human–humanoid barrier. Yet radically, sex between human Ayla and Neanderthal Broud results in a baby. Human and Neanderthal, then, are not so distinct.

Both novels examine the idea of the "dead end," evolutionary blind alleys that are hard to appreciate if we cleave to rigid models of "fitness" and metaphysical concepts of Nature. From the point of view of Auel's Clan, the human Ayla and her son are monstrously deformed. Even the tolerant medicine woman Iza, inheritor of a threadbare matriarchal tradition, offers to kill the boy.[155] The Clan's encounter with Ayla and her pregnancy via her rapist Broud force upon the most intelligent ones (Ayla and the medicine man, Creb) the conclusion that they must be generated through sex, not by spirits battling in an unseen world. The encounter with the strange stranger provokes science and thus a loss of "world," for which Ayla is scapegoated. When Broud becomes leader of the Clan, he instantly banishes Ayla out of murderous envy.

"He is a horse that thinks!" In his disturbing lyrical ballad "The Idiot Boy," Wordsworth describes a horse leading Johnny, a mentally disabled boy, through the forest.[156] Darwin remarks on reason in mules, finding it "even in animals very low in the scale of nature."[157] Wordsworth juxtaposes a less intelligent human with an intelligent nonhuman. The idiot boy is riding to fetch the doctor for his mother, a mission he never completes. The thinking horse resembles the thinking body of the old man traveling in "Animal Tranquillity." The boy's mother, Betty Foy, and the narrator, must detect this "thinking" in the horse's body—unless they can speak horse. Meanwhile, the idiot boy grins and burbles. His body doesn't speak: it just exists, inertly spasming. The tale is as inertial as Johnny. Many have deemed "The Idiot Boy" an idiot poem.[158] Johnny loses his way in the forest, and the narrator wonders halfheartedly whether he is going on some picaresque adventure. There is an unsettling blank at the heart of the poem, as Johnny and the horse wander aimlessly.

Wordsworth takes us to a zero level of living beingness and to a subaesthetic level, a place that isn't pretty. He confronts us with strange strangers—discharged soldiers, blind beggars, grief-crazed mothers.[159]

Sometimes the environmentalist passion for "animals" leapfrogs over these difficult strangers. The ecological thought thinks the strange stranger as the other mind, the other person, the neighbor, to use the Judeo-Christian term ("Love thy neighbor as thyself"). The ultimate neighbor is the zombielike "Müsselman" of the Nazi concentration camps, so resigned to fate that she or he appears to have lost the will to live or communicate in a "human" way.[160] Modern society has horrifying methods for reducing humans to a barely functioning zero level of aliveness, "vegetables" on life support or state terror victims, reduced to being "lower than dogs." Only consider Pope John Paul II's and President George Bush's so-called culture of life.[161] The CIA code word "rendition," used to describe the transporting of "terror suspects" to countries that torture, resembles the word for melting down the bones and marrow of livestock for glue and pet food.[162] If environmentalism means biopower—if "reducing" humans to animals means reducing animals to vegetables—the ecological thought wants nothing to do with it.

The boy speaks something like a poem at the haunting close of "The Idiot Boy": "The cocks did crow to-whoo, to-whoo, / And the sun did shine so cold" (lines 460–461). Compare Stephen Foster's "Oh! Susanna": "It rained all night the day I left, the weather it was dry, / The sun so hot, I froze to death, Susanna don't you cry" (lines 7–8).[163] While some discover miraculous imagination in lines like these—out of the mouths of babes—I can't help hearing the record of unspeakable suffering. In "Oh! Susanna," the speaker's journey has driven her or him mad—is he or she a runaway slave, as Foster's original lyrics suggest? Johnny patently doesn't understand his world. The images of freezing sunshine are records of pain. Icy fire is Petrarch's image of love on the brink of insanity. At the place where the strange stranger appears, there are intensities we can't understand. Wordsworth manages to exit the aesthetic without losing contact with perception. He takes us into a world of confusion and stupid suffering. All we can offer here is care and concern.

The ecological thought contemplates a subaesthetic level of being, beyond the cute and beyond the awesome. We can't call it beautiful (self-contained, harmonious) or sublime (awe-inspiring, open). This level unsettles and disgusts. It doesn't mirror our fantasies. It isn't hard to love Nature as a reflection of oneself. It isn't hard to love Nature as an

awe-inspiring open space. It's far harder to love the disturbing, disgusting beings who do not so easily wear a human face. Some of these beings
are human. One task of the ecological thought is to figure out how to
love the inhuman: not just the nonhuman (that's easier) but the radically
strange, dangerous, even "evil." For the inhuman is the strangely strange
core of the human.

This inhuman core swirls at the heart of Coleridge's *The Rime of the
Ancient Mariner:*

The moving Moon went up the sky,
And no where did abide:
Softly she was going up,
And a star or two beside—

Her beams bemocked the sultry main,
Like April hoar-frost spread;
But where the ship's huge shadow lay,
The charmed water burnt alway
A still and awful red.

Beyond the shadow of the ship,
I watched the water snakes:
The moved in tracks of shining white,
And when they reared, the elfish light
Fell off in hoary flakes.

Within the shadow of the ship
I watched their rich attire:
Blue, glossy green, and velvet black,
They coiled and swam; and every track
Was a flash of golden fire.

O happy living things! no tongue
Their beauty might declare:
A spring of love gushed from my heart,
And I blessed them unaware:
Sure my kind saint took pity on me,
And I blessed them unaware.

The selfsame moment I could pray;
And from my neck so free
The Albatross fell off, and sank
Like lead into the sea.

(4.263–291)[164]

Somehow the Ancient Mariner, tormented by fiendish spirits and disgusting life, manages to bless the water snakes "unaware," as if unconsciously.
There are several mutually exclusive interpretations of "O happy living
things! no tongue / Their beauty might declare" (282–283). Perhaps the
Mariner is exclaiming spontaneously. We hear this in the "O" at the start
of the line. The Mariner appreciates the snakes for no reason. The phrase,
"no tongue / Their beauty might declare" could mean "They were inde-
scribably beautiful," or "It was impossible to describe them as beautiful."
Could something be so sweet that it's sickly? Could something be so
beautiful that it's ugly? Or is the ugliness, or the beauty, strictly unspeakable? There is an openness here. It would be disastrous to maintain that
the Mariner blesses the snakes only unconsciously. It would mean we could
only ever perform groundbreaking actions if we're already wired for them.
Coleridge wants the issue to be more open-ended: "unaware" doesn't mean
"mindlessly" or "automatically."[165]

The time-lapse lines about the Moon slow down like clotting blood.
Experience becomes richer, more painful, more blissful, more uncertain.
In depression, we experience time slowing. We feel heavy, literally and
figuratively. We're forced into a contemplative space, but it isn't pretty.
Surely this is what any genuine meditative experience feels like. We become conscious in a situation where we have been acting unconsciously.
It's bound to be ugly and painful. We fall into the gravity well of depression. Where there is no hope, there is no fear. For a moment, there is absolute openness—"O happy living things!" This doesn't guarantee that
we're out of the well. In the Mariner's case, there are several hundred
lines of mind-bending horror to go.

Kant would call the openness aesthetic appreciation, beyond concept.
It certainly is this way for the Mariner, but in a manner that is stranger
than Kant intended. We can't call the Mariner's experience aesthetic.
It's experience in its sheer, traumatic rawness. To appreciate beautiful

things properly, we have to learn to spit out ugly things. In a sense, good bourgeois taste is about (as Captain Beefheart puts it) how to vomit beautifully.[166] But the Mariner doesn't spit out the snakes. How can he? He is frozen. This is a mutation of Kant. It is profoundly purposeless. The Mariner gains nothing from his appreciation—that is, until he can pray and the albatross slips from his neck, in a moment of blessed relief. The snakes themselves have no purpose: they just coil and swim. Their beauty (or incredible ugliness) is pointless and aimless, with their "tracks" like snail trails or the drips of an abstract painter, fireworks of slime.[167]

Appreciation for no reason may be an experience not of beauty but of ugliness, not of happiness but of compassion. Instead of bypassing it, the ecological thought seeps into the aesthetic dimension. It makes room for what we call, inadequately, the subjective and subjectivity.

LET ME TAKE YOU DOWN

The ecological thought realizes that all beings are interconnected. This is the mesh. The ecological thought realizes that the boundaries between, and the identities of, beings are affected by this interconnection. This is the strange stranger. The ecological thought finds itself next to other beings, neither me nor not-me. These other beings exist, but they don't really exist. They are strange, all the way down. The more intimately we know them, the stranger they become. The ecological thought is intimacy with the strangeness of the stranger. The ultimate strangeness, the strangeness of pure semblance, is (feminine) subjectivity, whose essence is radical passivity.[168] Interdependence is the coexistence between passivity and passivity. The zero social level is this sheer coexistence.

Intimacy is never so obvious as when we're depressed. Melancholy is the earth humor, made of black bile, the earth element. Melancholy art, such as the German "suffering play" (Trauerspiel), speaks the truth of pain.[169] This art might be more ecological than sunnier versions. To be intimate with the strange stranger is to be in various kinds of pain. Being glued to a heating world that might overwhelm or kill us is bad news. Ecology is stuck between melancholy and mourning. Nature language is like melancholy: holding on to a "bad" object, a toxic mother whose distance and objectlike qualities are venerated.[170] Environmentalism is a work of mourning for a mother we never had. To have ecology, we must give up Nature. But since we have been addicted to Nature for so long, giving up will be painful. Giving up a fantasy is harder than giving up a reality.

The attitude of Nature worship is like a depressed closeted gay man who insists he is straight.[171] Melancholy has a "sickly" quality of excessive devotion, excessive fidelity to the darkness of the present moment. Yet isn't this excessive fidelity exactly what we need right now? Dark ecology oozes through despair. Being realistic is always refreshing. Depression is the most accurate way of experiencing the current ecological disaster.[172] It's better than wishful thinking. Through dark ecology, we discover that ecology is everywhere our minds go. We don't have to think special thoughts, in a special way, to be ecological.

Even at the limit of dualism, we encounter ecology. Descartes argued that animals were unfeeling machines that humans could vivisect with impunity. Descartes promoted a dualism of subject and object that many consider to be one of the bases of ecological catastrophe. But Descartes himself begins the *Meditations* with the idea of an environment: he is sitting comfortably by a fire, holding the very page we're reading.[173] Doubt, intrinsic to the ecological thought, starts as a thought by that fire—is this really me? How can I tell? These aren't thoughts we should banish from an ecological society. Far from being the death knell of human harmony with the world, Descartes' doubting mind is profoundly ecological. There is more faith in honest doubt when it comes to feeling our way around the ecological thought, like a blind person.

Ecology exists in the thinking of Kant, who held that the human mind radically transcends its material conditions. When he imagines the power of the sublime to open our minds to the powers of reason, Kant envisions measuring a tree by the height of a man. The tree becomes a way of measuring a mountain; mountains measure the diameter of Earth; Earth measures the Milky Way. And the Milky Way measures what Kant calls the "the immense multitude of such Milky Way systems."[174] Soaring from a tree to the immensity of space like Milton, Kant performs the vastness of the ecological thought.

Darwin muses on Kant's amazement at the concept of duty—where did it come from, if the world is built on selfish competition? There must be a good reason for it. Perhaps in duty we glimpse the first stirrings of transpersonal, trans-species altruism. If humans are going to keep on going, we had better figure out how to transcend our impulses. There are too many books that worry about what "attitude" to assume toward "animals." Try substituting "Jews" or "immigrants" for "animals" and see whether these discussions of "the animal question" still sound palatable. It would be better to have no attitude at all. The strange stranger is beyond attitude, beyond ontology. This is why the ecological thought flows past nihilism. The assertion "there is nothing" supposes an audience of at least one (other) being. The ecological thought subverts idealism, since the position from which we can be idealists is coexistence.[175] It flows under materialism, for though evolution is palpably algorithmic—"let the strongest live and the weakest die"—this doesn't rule out the infinite responsibility of conscious beings to others.[176] The ecological thought finds its way out of a labyrinth of beliefs. Worrying about whether we're being stewards or tyrants or pilots of Spaceship Earth is window dressing. If we have a future, we will have decided to look after all sentient beings.

This decision is not calculating or utilitarian. At its limit, it is love. The trouble with love is that it has a tinge of "evil" about it. Out of the universe of things, as I wrote previously, I select you. Let's return to the beginning of Chapter 1. Isn't this the trouble with "Earthrise" and Google Earth? Something lurks in the supposed innocence and wonder of "Earthrise," something that Google Earth makes clearer. When I can see my mother's fishpond in her garden in Wimbledon, London, from my desk in Davis, California, there no longer exists a world "over there." What I see is what I wish to see: I can't subtract my own desire to see from the parts of Earth I'm seeing. It's like that scene in Hitchcock's *The Birds:* we see the burning Bodega Bay from above, then birds begin to fill the screen, as if this supposedly neutral "bird's-eye view" has been filled in with malicious intent.[177] The bird's-eye view selects Earth out of all the other places in the universe—there's no place like home. This view is far from neutral—or worse, its very neutrality may be part of its evil. The decision to care for all sentient beings is an admission of the evil that is our big picture gaze. This is the soil in which dark ecology grows. Tree hugging begins to sound sinister, not innocent. Yet we have to go through this darkness. It's the only way to grow up. If we don't take responsibility this way, we're stuck in an attitude we can never shake off, in the damaged and damaging attitude that gave birth to the ecological thought.

3
Forward Thinking

The mirrors of the gigantic shadows which futurity casts upon the present

Percy Shelley

Environmentalism is often apocalyptic. It warns of, and wards off, the end of the world. The title of Rachel Carson's *Silent Spring* says it all.[1] But things aren't like that: the end of the world has already happened. We sprayed the DDT. We exploded the nuclear bombs. We changed the climate. This is what it looks like after the end of the world. Today is not the end of history. We're living at the beginning of history. The ecological thought thinks forward. It knows that we have only just begun, like someone waking up from a dream.

We're responsible for global warming. Formally responsible, whether or not we caused it, whether or not we can prove that we caused it. We're responsible for global warming simply because we're sentient. No more elaborate reason is required. If you believe a more elaborate reason is required, consider the following:

When you see a child about to be hit by a truck, do you protest, "I'm not directly responsible for her death, so I won't help her"? When your house is burning down, do you say, "Well, I didn't start the fire, so I'm not responsible for putting it out"? The big difference is that unlike the girl and the house, you can't see climate. Climate isn't weather. You can see weather, but not climate, in the same way that you can't see momentum but you can see velocity. Climate is a derivative of weather. Very powerful computers using terabytes of RAM can barely model climate.

You can't really point to climate, but it exists. It doesn't matter if it snowed somewhere, just as it doesn't matter if a truck that's about to run you down is slowing down or speeding up. If it has enough momentum to kill you, it's going to do so unless you get out of the way. If you're watching a little girl in front of that moving truck, you're obliged to rescue her, for the simple reason that you can see her. In other words, simply because we're sentient—let's set the bar low to ensure that even snails and the snailiest humans are also responsible—we're obliged to address global warming. No proof is required that we caused it—looking for absolute proof inhibits our response.

This is tough: taking responsibility for something you can't see. But it's no tougher than taking responsibility for, say, not killing—you don't have to come up with a reason; you just do it and figure out why later. That's why it's called an ethical decision. It doesn't have to be proved or justified. You just do it. This doesn't mean that your act is unconscious. By no means am I advising us just to do what we feel to be right. It means that one can act spontaneously and consciously. I'll discuss this seeming paradox in a moment.

Global warming denial depends upon and contributes to an idea of Nature not that different from a certain attitude to the child in the street or the burning house: "It's over there—in some fundamental way, it's not my concern." Part of assuming direct responsibility for global warming will be abandoning the idea of Nature, an ideological barrier to realizing how everything is interconnected. Global warming deniers are like a man with a gun to someone's head, saying, "Give me a good reason not to shoot this guy." Do you give a good reason ("It's right, it feels good, there's a symbiotic web in which we're immersed and you're damaging it, you're upsetting a natural balance . . ."), or assuming you're strong enough, do you just grab the gun?

All the reasons in the world aren't reason enough, from a certain point of view. This is why Søren Kierkegaard argues that the "ethical" position is a step up from the "aesthetic" one—in the aesthetic one, you do things because they feel nice or because they look nice. In the ethical one, niceness—or even rational soundness, which is perhaps also a kind of aesthetic order—doesn't matter. In a perverse way, environmentalist arguments based on consequentialism (e.g., it makes you feel better to care for Earth) actually impede action, as we shall see.

One implication is that it's possible to be fully conscious and totally spontaneous, at the same time and for the same reasons. I disagree with Gregory Bateson, who asserts that the only good decisions are unconscious ones, an idea that sounds suspiciously, like "The only good woman is a dead one."[2] This disagreement affects our interpretations of a key moment in Coleridge's poem *The Rime of the Ancient Mariner*, explored in the previous chapter. What the Mariner performs with the water snakes isn't just a random brain firing, nor is it even all that unusual, if we have the eyes to see it. Greeting a stranger is a form of "blessing unaware" (4.285–287)—we don't know them when we say hello.[3] "Unaware" doesn't have to mean "automatically"—if it did, we would be at risk of an infinite regress, for who or what installed the "blessing software" that allowed this act to occur automatically?

The ecological thought spreads out in both time and space, but thinking big doesn't contradict being intimate. A mesh that prevented us from imagining the strange stranger wouldn't be a mesh, and vice versa. Ecology is about relating not to Nature but to aliens and ghosts. Intimacy presents us with the problem of inner space. Our intimacy with other beings is full of ambiguity and darkness. Strange strangers flow and dissimulate. If we edit out the ambiguity and darkness, we achieve nothing but aggression.

The ecological thought is dark but not suicidal. The "into the wild" meme plays no part. Once we discover the void at our hearts, we can't remain indifferent to the strange stranger. The discovery itself is a form of care. It is far more affirming to wake up in the darkness of the ecological thought than to continue dreaming of life destroyed forever. Ecoapocalypse is always for someone. It presupposes an audience. What kinds of sadistic "you asked for it" fantasies does it promote?[4] To what extent does it leave everything the same as it ever was, the day before the day after tomorrow? It seems that for many people, it's easier to imagine the end of the world than to imagine the end of capitalism. The more one thinks the ecological thought, the more one realizes that the "let it be" mentality (no human "interference" with the environment, no "anthropo-centric" care for "animals," and so on) is just the flip side of laissez-faire ideology. They look so different, but they are really the same thing seen from different sides, as if subject to parallax.[5] The global banking crisis of 2008 should alert us (it even alerted Federal Reserve Chairman Alan Greenspan) to the truth that "let it be" economics is an ideological fan-tasy. Financial deregulation made the stock market appear "natural," like a cloud. When it collapsed, it stopped being a "thing over yonder"—a rei-fied process that just happens. America and the United Kingdom have left the era of "stuff happens" (how U.S. Secretary of Defense Donald Rums-feld described looting and anarchy in the streets of Baghdad after the in-vasion of Iraq).

The ultimate horizon of ecology goes beyond capitalism, though capi-talism will definitely pass through a green phase. In its junkie-like search for the next stock market high, capitalism will create a green bubble. But capitalism isn't the terminus of four and a half billion years of replication. Capitalism marks only the beginning of thinking the ecological thought beyond our personal backyard. Versions of ecology adapted to serve the interests of corporations are temporary distortions. Capitalism shows only the truth of cooperation. Community we inherit; we have to choose cooperation. The factory system enabled workers to choose to cooperate with each other by throwing them together, turning them into replace-able parts of replaceable machines.[6] We inhabit a gigantic network of in-terlocking mechanical structures that become increasingly detailed and increasingly global. Ever more intricate cages appear in which we can recognize each other as conscious beings capable of choosing. The first realization of a conscious being is that she has been asleep, in a cage. We must abandon a Romantic ecology of community. To imagine ecological society as community is to inhibit future cooperation, because "commu-nity" language appeals to fantasies about a historical moment before the idea of socialism had appeared.[7]

Thinking cooperation widely and deeply is an obligation of the eco-logical thought. All strange strangers are already cooperating. In my hometown (Davis, California), there are thousands of crows who use the cars and streets as a nutcracker. They harvest walnuts from the trees that line a particular road; they fly up; when a car drives past, they drop the walnuts so precisely that they fall just in front of the oncoming wheels. There are monkeys in Delhi who should probably learn how to pay for their frequent bus rides (perhaps with fruit?). If you can't beat 'em, join 'em. A globalized world means that the awful charity song "We Are the World" includes the sentient beings, the coral, the trees.[8]

I would smile to see chimpanzees walking dogs down the street and countries adopting ethical rules for the treatment of robots. I would enjoy a movement toward greater vegetarianism, as long as that doesn't mean an increase in the furious, erotic hatred of the body that manifests in "veganorexia" and size zero clothing. I hope governments decide to cover every roof in the world with solar panels. I would like us not to ponder whether "animals" have rights but to respond to the demands of coexistent beings. Most of all I'll be glad if the effect of the climate disruption crisis is not upgraded capitalism but a long hard look at why we're alive and what we want to do about it, together.

THE CULTURAL LOGIC OF EARLY ENVIRONMENTALISM

Are there any signs in the artistic tealeaves? The title of this section parodies Fredric Jameson's treatise, *Postmodernism, or, The Cultural Logic of Late Capitalism.*[9] We may look back on postmodernism and decide that it marked the beginning of environmental global culture. Postmodernism was the moment at which global capital and the totally administered world made it impossible (in a highly toxic, negative, destructive way) not to detect the mesh. Postmodernism's localism, the pastiche, the "micronarratives," point to something they refer to in their absence, a system (or is it?), a world (can we still use this word?), an environment—for want of a better term—stunningly vast and disturbingly decentered. In a world of "full spectrum dominance" and the colonization of the Moon and Mars, where does the environment stop—does that mean it's not really an environment anymore?[10] The logic of capital has made sure that the environment certainly isn't what we have been calling Nature any more.

Environmentalism and postmodernism appear to be opposites. One is "artificial," the other "natural." One is about human products, the other about nonhuman being. One involves buying organic; the other implies celebrating artifice. One likes integration and authenticity; the other likes disintegration and pastiche. Yet postmodernism and environmentalism are really two sides of the same historical moment. Take the music of David Byrne and Laurie Anderson. Early postmodern theory likes to think of them as nihilists or relativists, bricoleurs in the bush of ghosts. Laurie Anderson's "O Superman" features a repeated sample of her voice and a sinister series of recorded messages.[11] This voice typifies postmodern art materials: forms of incomprehensible, unspeakable existence. Some might call it inert, sheer existence—art as ooze. It's a medium in which meaning and unmeaning coexist. This oozy medium has something physical about it, which I call ambience.[12] Anderson's voice provides a taste of something that is disturbingly just "there." Likewise, David Byrne's and Brian Eno's song "The Overload" talks of "A terrible signal, / Too weak to even recognize" (lines 1–2).[13] The signal is either very weak, very frightening, or both. Its very weakness is what is terrible about it. It is a weird reminder of something that the domination of life forms has both uncovered and forgotten.

Hiding in plain sight in postmodern art is the mesh. When we go into Giuseppe Penone's room filled with bags of dry bay leaves at the Pompidou Centre, or look at the way Dan Flavin adjusts space with fluorescent light, or see the biomorphic, swelling sculptures of Louise Bourgeois, or hear the intense timbres of Eliane Radigue, we become aware of an environment. And because causality works backward, we can look back and see that what was eluding us was there all the time, in the space around the words of Mallarmé, in the huge swathes of color Turner paintings, in the way Japanese court music is so attuned to the space of ceremony that it seems to be listening to itself.

Ambience points to where we are right now. We are here. Keith Rowe, guitarist of the free improvisation band AMM, says that silence in music is "un-intention." The blank page, the open canvas, the gallery space, the silence (or quiet or, more properly, noise) around and within the music displays the medium in which and through which we're reading, listening, looking, participating.[14] Ambience is the extended phenotype of the poem, the way in which the text and the environment develop together—the "extended phenotext."[15]

In the spaces ambience opens up, we see history—Nature is just the rei-
fied, plasticized version. "Here" is a mesh of entangled presences and
absences, not a foundational, localist, antiglobal concept. "Here" contains
difference. Ambience points us to the here and now, in a compelling way
that goes beyond explicit content—we don't have to dig whales or mountains but can literally be here, now, with the artwork. And ambience opens
up our ideas of space and place into a radical questioning.

Capitalism has brought all life forms together, if only in the negative.
The ground under our feet is being changed forever, along with the water
and air. So along with the political radicalisms that seek to create new
forms of collectivity out of the crisis of climate disruption, there must also
be a rigorous and remorseless theoretical radicalism that opens our minds
to where we are, about the fact that we're here. This radicalism is almost
religious in its passionate intensity.[16] Perhaps postmodern art and philosophy were the heavy digging for the emerging ecological constellation.
Yet the words "environment" and "environmentalism" aren't right to describe this. First, in a world where we truly cared for what we now call the
environment, there would be no need to point it out as such. We would be
it in the most radical sense. Second, a religious vocabulary is risky: it
might set up ecology as another kind of superbeing outside the mesh, outside the obvious impermanence and evanescence of reality.

Is the ecological thought just a killjoy, then? What's wrong with the
"re-enchantment of the world"? There's nothing wrong with enchant-
ment. It's the prefix "re-" that's the source of the problem. This prefix
assumes that the world was once enchanted, that we have done something
to disenchant it, and that we can, and should, get back to where we once
belonged. We simply can't unthink modernity. If there is any enchant-
ment, it lies in the future. The ecological "enchants the world," if en-
chantment means exploring the profound and wonderful openness and
intimacy of the mesh. What can we make of the new constellation? What
art, literature, music, science, and philosophy are suitable to it? Art can
contain utopian energy. As Percy Shelley put it, art is a kind of shadow
from the future that looms into our present world.[17]

Environmental art as we know it will cease to exist at some point in the
history of the ecological thought. For one thing, ecological art will exit
the elegiac mode.[18] Ecological elegies will wither or mutate. Elegies are

about burying the dead.[19] They are the grief equivalent of canned laughter: they do the mourning for you, thus providing an outlet for one's sadistic fantasies against the lost one. Nature elegy is a paradox, as it's about losing something we never really had: losing a fantasy, not a reality. Perhaps a new form of paradoxical elegy will arise. What ecological art will certainly not be able to get away with for very much longer is happy-happy-joy-joy eco-sincerity.[20] This mode will look less and less relevant, and less and less reverent, the further up to our necks we get in our own waste. The ecological thought demonstrates that the aesthetic dimension is full of emptiness—gaps and openness—rather than being a solid, plastic thing. It has no authority. So ecological art is an art of "whateverness."[21] It might be photographic rather than painterly, if by "painterly" we mean objets d'art with their aura of specialness and distance, floating in some museum like products in a shop window.[22] Some contemporary environmental art is like an aura without an object. Beyond even this, the art will be about "unworking" rather than about the precious *work* of art as such.[23] This will foreshadow a future society based on the "whateverness" of the strange stranger, a society of hospitality and responsibility.

There are three directions for ecological art. The first emphasizes automated processes such as evolution. Art that uses algorithms fit into this category: serialism, diastic poetry, even abstract expressionism.[24] This is the art of letting be (German: *Gelassenheit*): "Let the chips fall where they may." The artist sets up some parameters, starts the process, and watches what happens. The second approach emphasizes consciousness, being caught in the headlights of our awareness of the mesh. The art is ironic, full of darkness and unfathomable depths and deceptive shallows. The third approach is about the ruthless way in which mathematics and other sciences are now able to model so-called Nature: think of modern cinematic special effects. These three approaches could manifest in the same work of art.

Let's begin by looking at technical and scientific innovation in art. These innovations, such as zooming, stop motion, time-lapse, and the use of fractal geometry to generate clouds, mountains, explosions (you name it), open up the mesh for inspection. Such techniques can recreate an arty aura that evokes feelings of distance, as any student with a poster of the Mandelbrot set on her wall could tell you. But in the main they serve the admirable purpose of demystifying our planet and our Universe—even that kitschy poster has something nicely uncool about it. We saw that you can write an algorithm that codes for plants and flowers. You can also write algorithms that code for mountains, clouds, and so on. Benoit Mandelbrot discovered that supposedly random patterns in Nature consist of fractals.[25] Fractal shapes seem irregular at first, but on closer inspection they reveal a clear structure based on iterating algorithmic processes. These processes map onto themselves with a fractional ratio, creating jagged, complexly folded, crinkly forms that are self-similar—you can cut a little piece out of them, and it will resemble the main shape. This is quite different from the whole being greater than the sum of its parts (holism): it's all parts, all the way up and all the way down, so that a "higher" level (say, the relative height of trees in a forest) maps onto "lower" levels (say, the relative width of branches in a single tree).

To have holism, there must be a clear difference between a top level and other, lower, levels of the pattern. No difference means no whole separate from the parts. Fractal geometry denatures Nature. If you can plot the coastline of Britain using well-formed algorithms, or generate a computer graphic of a shower of molten lava from an image of a simple linear jet (as in *Star Wars: Revenge of the Sith*), then Nature, as a solid, comprehension-defying thing "over yonder," has evaporated.

Art in an age of fractal geometry strips the aura from Nature. Yet more profound mysteries emerge: the mesh and the strange stranger. Scientific instruments, such as contact microphones placed on a window, can allow us to hear things such as standing waves over the Pacific Ocean: art as a form of data collection.[26] This brings us to the art of letting be, since we could imagine technology as bringing phenomena to light. In an age of movies, close-ups and zooming allow us to see inside and around things. In an age of powerful processors, fractal geometry reveals fuzzy, crinkly things that used to seem organic, subject to some mysterious living principle.

The experimental movies of Stan Brakhage, with their flickering colors induced by painting onto the film stock, are profoundly environmental. Psychogeography, the practice invented by Guy Debord and the Situationists of Paris 1968 fame, reclaims the environment through the *dérive*, or "drifting," aimless wandering. Debord explicitly states that psychogeography is ecological. The *dérive* is "a technique of rapid passage through varied ambiances."[27] Work by David Robertson, Richard Long, and Hamish Fulton falls into this category. In a way, psychogeography is like the indigenous Australian walkabout. Perhaps ecological projects such as installing solar panels are a form of Situationism.

Virginia Woolf's narratives are ecological because, unlike Joyce and Lawrence, who also developed "stream of consciousness" techniques, Woolf lets consciousnesses slide into each other: this includes nonhuman as well as human consciousnesses. Consider the extraordinary passage in *Mrs. Dalloway* where two old women watch a skywriting plane:

> There's a fine young feller aboard of it, Mrs. Dempster wagered, and away and away it went, fast and fading, away and away the aeroplane shot; soaring over Greenwich and all the masts; over the little island of grey churches, St. Paul's and the rest till, on either side of London, fields spread out and dark brown woods where adventurous thrushes hopping boldly, glancing quickly, snatched the snail and tapped him on a stone, once, twice, thrice.[28]

Woolf's control (or, better, careful lack of control) of indirect speech lets us flow in and out of characters' heads—one of which is surely the thrush. In a single sentence, we go up and away, then out to "either side" of the city (which side?), then, incredibly, into the intense attention of the thrush tapping the shell. It's as if Woolf's prose zooms in and out as ruthlessly as a movie camera. In the middle of another novel, *To the Lighthouse*, Woolf places a chapter called "Time Passes," which describes the subtle physical shifts and play of light and darkness in and around a house deserted by the novel's characters.[29] The environment as such comes to the forefront. The fact that the reader is made aware of the house and its environs without the characters doesn't exactly bestow on the reader any power of knowing something the characters don't know. What this description does, rather, is undermine the idea that the house is a neutral stage set on which the characters act. The existentially vivid presence of the house, its meaningless material inertia, emerges.

Environmental art must deeply explore materiality. There are poems that, like music, experiment with tones and timbres—the very matter and energy out of which sound is made. Caroline Bergvall's *Goan Atom* series is a powerful example.[30] La Monte Young experimented with "just intonation," designing tones that include many more, and more highly varied, sounds (harmonics) than the traditional equal temperament and Christian-derived ones.[31] Experiments with pure color in painting are environmental, such as Yves Klein's luminous blues (the YKB series). Eliane Radigue designs very long synthesizer sounds that open up the space in which they are played.[32] Alvin Lucier experiments with the way resonance is about the material out of which sound comes and the material environment in which sounds vibrate.[33] John Cage's *4′ 33″* is deliberately environmental, as its four and a half minutes' silence was written for an open-air amphitheater.

Happenings and raves are environmental, from London's 1967 14-Hour Technicolour Dream to the acid house of 1988 on. House music is viral: it's made of strings of musical code, often sampled, strung together. These strings mutate frequently and can easily be spliced into other house tracks. House tracks are not complete in themselves (also like viruses) but form sections of longer sequences mixed by a DJ. This viral organization repeats at other levels. The music sequences rapidly organized an ever-growing mass of dancing limbs. Utopian combinations of gay and straight, black and white, upper class and working class, made possible the idea of collectivity, the idea of joining hands toward the lasers in the sound factory (as one famous club was called), after a decade in which Prime Minister Margaret Thatcher insisted that "society doesn't exist." It was situational and, in its way, Situationist. The Mutoid Waste Company recycled materials to create new décor. Music sampling became faster, cheaper, and easier, and DJing is the equivalent of a musical *dérive.* There were themes of globalism and a new collective dreamtime called virtual reality—what was it? We can tar house music with the brush of hindsight as the vanguard of the new world order, where globalization and the Internet keep everyone slaving away. But as the initial rush of euphoria wears off, there remains utopian energy in the idea of exploring differences in collectivity.

Improvisation introduces Darwinism into art. Keith Rowe's "unintention" takes place when something happens that we conventionally call silence. If all sounds—and nonsounds—are included, everything is "intended." The practice of improvisation stretches "intention" from its usual connotations of deliberateness, even away from the philosophical assumption that consciousness is "intentional" (it is always "consciousness of . . .").

Free jazz is about adaptation, since one instrument depends completely on another, and all instruments depend on the "environment" of "unintention" around them. This music listens to itself, following the brilliant theory of musical evolution, apocryphally attributed to Miles Davis: "Sometimes you have to play a long time to be able to play like yourself."

Because of this listening quality, free jazz can be highly contemplative. The guitarist Allan Holdsworth sees the guitar fret board as a field of possibilities like an abacus.[34] When he solos, Holdsworth tries out every possibility relating to the key signature of a tune, some closer to the basic harmony, others further away. Improvisation is adaptation plus awareness. Holdsworth is the finest and most virtuosic guitarist of the early twenty-first century, but he is utterly modest and humble, unlike some of his peers.[35] So it goes with the contemplative, listening quality of his music. There's something contemplative about the ecological thought. When you think about adaptation, it is like music that listens to itself. This form of awareness foreshadows a future society in which introversion and passivity have a key role to play. Perhaps the ecological art of the future will deal with passivity and weakness; with lowliness, not loftiness.

And now for *noir*. Paul Chaney's *The Lonely Now* documents the way our mind can't tear itself from the mesh but drowns within it, fully conscious: "In *Vole—No Pulse* [a video work], a small rodent accidentally killed by a lawnmower turns out to be pregnant, giving rise to the kind of horrifically irresolvable moral dilemma common to any agricultural endeavour. . . . Install incubators? Open an orphanage . . . ?"[36] The video documents the loving burial of the vole in a special graveyard. Then there's the lovingly small model of a farmhouse, a little fragment of place in an ocean of space. There's "Slug-o-Metric," a device that measures slugs while killing them.

Comora Tolliver's "Pod" is an installation about seed banks.[37] Many countries store their seeds in banks so that the genomes won't cease to exist if there is a war or a natural disaster.[38] Corporations such as Monsanto have made it almost impossible to rely on age-old methods of saving seeds, having copyrighted the genomes of plants such as soy. Tolliver's work shows how all beings exist together in a space that is itself a product of their existence. Tolliver lines her installation space with highly reflective, artificial-looking Mylar: its folds and creases induce a hypnotic intensity, the visual equivalent of a wall of guitar feedback. In the center is an egglike structure, also coated with Mylar, inside which is a gravelike space that contains dead flowers in a pool of water. This is dark ecology, indeed.[39] Photographs of paint oozing down the mirrorlike Mylar disturb our sense of foreground and background. The trails of paint look almost three-dimensional, as if they are tendrils that grow downward from above the photo frame, some distance in front of the Mylar's surface. Rather than resolving our disorientation, Tolliver's work heightens our sense of how the ecological crisis has disrupted our normative sense of foreground and background.

Remember a suggestion in the Introduction, that what I'm aiming at is an upgraded version of animism. Ancient animisms treat beings as people, without a concept of Nature. I'm going to cross out this word to prevent people from thinking of it as another belief system, in particular a system that implies something about living rather than nonliving things: ~~animism~~. Is there any art that points the way? Frankenstein and its best modern adaptation, *Blade Runner*, are perfect examples. So is *Solaris*, the novel by Stanislav Lem, and movies by Andrei Tarkovsky and Steven Soderbergh.[40]

Solaris is about falling in love with the strange stranger. Solaris is a distant sentient planet that tries to communicate with the human inhabitants of an orbiting space station. Its communications take the form of simulated, walking, talking versions of the inhabitants' darkest, guiltiest memories. Most go mad trying to ward off these simulations. But the psychologist Kris decides to do the almost impossible, to commit himself to the planet-mind, fully knowing that the simulation of his suicidal girlfriend is a mere illusion. In Tarkovsky's adaptation, Kris's descent onto the planet's surface isn't shown directly. The camera pans up and away from a small island on that surface, an island that the planet has made to look like Kris's childhood home. As the Bach soundtrack fades into organ and synthesizer discords, we see that the island floats in a gigantic, terrifying sea of pulsating colors and lights.[41] Kris appears marooned on a little island of psychic consistency in a psychotic ocean. It is also as if Kris has chosen to live on the surface of film itself, that liquid, oceanic medium of throbbing, streaming color and sound.

It might be impossible to design a machine that uses algorithms to make a choice between things that appear easy to discriminate, like the inside and outside of a set.[42] If all conscious beings are machines, do they still have strange strangeness? There is something amiss with the language of individualism: I am not a number; I am a free man![43] The argument that some mental phenomena aren't reducible to scientifically observable processes seems weak. It would be more effective to make a counterassertion at the level of the scientific real.[44] Persons are irreducible aspects of reality. Whether or not machines can think, we will soon confront the question the Korean government faced when it developed ethical rules for robots. Art has already stepped into the breach on this issue. Ridley Scott's film *Blade Runner* (based on Philip K. Dick's novel *Do Androids Dream of Electric Sheep?*) remains astonishing to think with.[45] It's about artificial life, "replicants" who work as slaves in extraterrestrial colonies. Their makers allow them four years of "life" after which they are "retired" (they run down or are killed). Their manufacturers install artificial memories to give them an illusory structure within which to base something like sanity.

Blade Runner is classic noir detective fiction, in which the detective Deckard finds out he is implicated in the crime. Noir is the mode of dark ecology: in it, we discover that the detective's personhood ironically contaminates the scene. Although he has been hired to "retire" some renegade replicants, Deckard himself is a replicant. Ecological awareness follows a similar path. Our ideas about having an objective point of view are part of the problem, as are ideological beliefs in immersion in a lifeworld. Deckard discovers something about the fragility and contingency of life when he falls in love with the replicant Rachel, the plaything of the CEO of the corporation that manufactures them. This fragility and contingency becomes even more intensely clear when at the end he is saved from a fall to death by the rebel replicant Roy. Roy gives a powerful, melancholy speech in which, like the Creature in *Frankenstein*, he owns his own death, in a moment that is both ethical and tragic: "I've . . . *seen* things you people wouldn't believe . . . Attack ships on fire off the shoulder of Orion . . . I've watched C-beams glitter in the darkness at Tannhäuser Gate . . . All those—moments—will be lost in time, like . . . tears in rain: time to die" (my transcription). Compare the Creature's last words: " 'But soon,' he cried, with sad and solemn enthusiasm, 'I shall die' . . . He was soon borne away by the waves, and lost in darkness and distance."[46] The profundity of *Blade Runner*, and of *Frankenstein*, isn't to point out that artificial life and intelligence are possible but that human life already is this artificial intelligence. Descartes tellingly referred to intelligence as the *res intellectus*, the "thing that thinks."[47]

What makes humans human is not some Natural or essential component of being but a relationship that can never be fulfilled. This asymmetrical relationship is perfectly captured when Roy goads his manufacturers in *Blade Runner*. Roy picks up a pair of eyes on which a scientist has been working: "If only you could see what I have seen . . . with your eyes" (my transcription). On the one hand, the eyes are physical things belonging to the Corporation; on the other hand, they reflect the mind of the replicant. This is one reason for the pathos of the heart of *Frankenstein*, in which the Creature narrates what he has seen with Frankenstein's eyes.

Blade Runner appreciates what makes *Frankenstein* disturbing: not the Creature's difference from but his similarity to human beings. In the language of the Enlightenment, the Creature is *humane*—essentially human. He displays humanity and pathos, mostly through his speech, which always strikes new readers as disturbing in its very dignity (mileage remains in the languages of personhood). His disgusting features contradict his noble eloquence. *Frankenstein* is a novel for our ecological times, more so than ever as we enter an age of genomics and nanotechnology. The common misreading of *Frankenstein* is that it warns against tampering with the "laws of Nature" or playing God.[48] This is how the arrogant Frankenstein would like to see things. The focus of the novel is in the gauntlet the Creature throws down to human beings. You think you are ethical? You think you are the wisest, smartest beings on Earth? Can you love and treat kindly a being as ugly as me, as uncertain in his status as a person as me? Can you forgive another being's violence, you who execute and torture in the name of justice and reason?

The uncanny truth is not that we're all the same, that underneath humans are not different from the working-class replicants who perform their dirty work. In their very humanity, humans are already replicants: beings with artificial cores, just a sum of memories. What if we could make artificial people? When does a human being become a person? Mary Shelley, Philip K. Dick, and Ridley Scott dramatize these questions, by taking them absolutely literally, in the best tradition of thought experiments. Philosopher Derek Parfit exploits science fiction's popularization of the thought experiment, when he imagines having his personality teleported into another body on another planet.[49] Even if we never teleport ourselves, even if artificial intelligence is strictly impossible, these are phenomena with which to think the ecological thought. They are like Milton's exploration of extraterrestrial life. We may never make contact with life on other planets. It's highly likely that alien life exists, however, and thinking about it is a significant aspect of thinking interconnection. As Levinas said, "the idea that I am sought out in the intersidereal spaces is not science fiction, but expresses my passivity as a self."[50]

FORWARD SCIENCE

Posthumanism (a current trend in the humanities) too glibly combines (1) a deconstruction of humanness—and animal-ness, and life form-ness—into sets of machine-like, algorithmic processes; and (2) decidedly nonreductionist, holistic, quasi-mystical systems theory.[51] In effect, posthumanism asserts, "There is a nonself" and "There is a non-nature." The ecological thought reserves a special place for the "subject"—the mind, the person, even the soul. Posthumanism seems suspiciously keen to delete the paradigm of humanness like a bad draft; yet "Humanism has to be denounced only because it is not sufficiently human."[52] Even worse is the Skinnerian behaviorism that says "Good riddance" to "man."[53] This is turning reductionism into a religion. It probably would be nice actually to have achieved something like humanness in the first place. What if being human is the encounter with the strange stranger—in other words, at a certain limit, an encounter with the inhuman?[54] Isn't this the very "posthumanism" for which some are yearning? Human beingness is already fissured from within.[55] Is the ecological thought an antihumanist or even antihuman thought? Posthumanism and deep ecology make strange bedfellows—the first believes in non-nature, the second in Nature—but they might find common cause on this: two legs bad, four legs better. Even though the ecological thought appears at first glance to have things in common with posthumanism, it ends up seeping through posthuman ideological barriers.

Finding out what all this means might imply more than installing a minimally functioning, though ultimately papery, ideological fantasy between ourselves and the void: though of course we should confront this void, it would also be helpful if we could know why to get up in the morning. So what we do as humanists isn't just about providing better PR for science. Along with figuring out what implications science has for society and so on, we should be in the business of asking scientists to do things for us. Humanists should create Web sites listing experiments they want done. My top suggestion would be exploring the question "Is consciousness intentional?" Negative results would provide a pretty good reason not to hurt life forms. If we could show that consciousness wasn't some lofty bonus prize for being elaborately wired but a default mode that came bundled with the software, then worms are conscious in every meaningful sense. A worm could become a Buddha, as a worm (paging Lowly). Are we sure nonhumans don't have a sense of "I"? Are we sure that we do?[56] One possible conclusion to be drawn from the difficulties of AI theory is that human brains are "too weak" to understand themselves.[57] In weakness is solidarity with strangers.

Humanists forging ahead with the ecological thought should step up and suggest experiments, based on their varied, complex, radical, and interestingly divergent ideas. And scientists should at least take a look. Here are some this book has proposed:

1. Can animals enjoy art?
2. Can animals self-reflect? Can humans self-reflect? Is self-reflection important regarding suffering?
3. What is awareness? Is it a "higher" (less frequent) or "lower" (more frequent) cognitive capacity?
4. Did Neanderthals have imagination? Do we? Does it matter?
5. Does AI suffer? Can bacteria suffer? What are the "lower" limits for suffering?
6. Is consciousness intentional?
7. Are thinking and perceiving discrete?

To get "ahead of the curve" enough to ask sensible questions, humanists must get over both atomism (especially the sort that thinks of atoms as hard little ping pong balls) and holism (especially the sort maintaining that wholes are different from their parts). This means rejecting, or putting on serious hold, most theories of Nature and post-Nature. Humanists must play the irritating Columbo-style guy at the back of the room, the one who asks the unanswerable question.

The profound implications of ecological theory present obstacles to their full acceptance. Materialism suggests that if the mind is reducible to the brain, then the brain is capable of being explained in terms of its physical causes—its "environment."[58] Cognitive abilities thus evolved like fingers or lungs. Your mind is an assemblage of duplicated and reduplicated processes that evolved unevenly. There may be no unified model for brain and mind. For instance, the human brain appears to be a kluge, a good-enough assemblage of different gadgets from different life forms.[59] Classical models of minds are transparent but may not work or are highly arbitrary, while "connectionist" models (advocated here) work, but they aren't transparent.[60] This may be because of something to do with the mind itself. The mind may not have hardwired rules for parsing reality. In order to understand the mind, we may have to make one first.

There might be "less" to consciousness than we suppose. AI theory tends to set the bar really high for poor computer programs. If I had to access a sense of self every time I did anything, my mind might freeze, or I might wind up in a mental hospital. You might not need a good picture of the world somewhere inside your head, or even a picture at all, to walk or play games or even think. Why is this relevant to the ecological thought? Cognitive science claims that cognition is about the mind's interaction with its world. Cognizing is fundamentally environmental. You wouldn't need to do it if you weren't in an environment. (This is almost tautological: you wouldn't exist at all if you didn't have an environment.) Jakob von Uexküll was onto this with his extraordinary hypotheses concerning the worlds (*Umwelten*) of animals such as ticks.[61] Yet as seen in Chapter 1, the world is "less than" rather than "greater than." Forget holism, organicism, and Heidegger, who maintains that human beings have a world, unlike the other poor saps who live here.[62] What a relief. This is excellent for the ecological thought, because it means ~~animism~~ isn't mystification. It also implies that the distinctly (and disturbingly) Germanic type of environmental language, sounding suspiciously like an anti-Semitic peasant during the Crusades, has been barking up the wrong tree. And in every sense that matters, living beings (and DNA, for that matter) have a world—just not much of one.

There are problems with connectionism, which is the cognitive-scientific view I'm outlining. The devil is in the details. Connectionism maintains that mental phenomena arise from interconnected processing systems. That is to say, there is no mind as such, because mind always emerges from interacting networks, at least one of which must be a system for processing inputs such as sensations and perceptions. But does this really add anything to our understanding? Saying that organisms "enact" their environment by interacting with it could be a simple inversion of saying that organisms have organs. To a hammer, everything looks like a nail. One could say, "The world has become hammerable" instead of "I am using a hammer." This already sounds a bit Heidegger-ish: it merely shunts our problems into a different area. An inside-out sock is still a sock.

Connectionist AI is excited that cognition may be reducible to an algorithm. But it's hard to resist imagining this algorithm as a tiny being, a sort of homunculus, already floating in an environmental "soup" of information—an infinite regress.[63] The explanation for organisms and environments is tinier organisms and tinier environments. If we can make sense of organisms as algorithms at this level, suggests Francisco Varela, just imagine the possibilities when we scale up to the level of brains, colossal sets of algorithmic calculating machines. Varela's argument implies that although we can reduce mental phenomena to mechanisms, the whole (brain) is greater than the sum of its parts. There is a both-and logic operating here. We can have tiny components and a big self: reductionism and holism at the same time.

The ecological thought must hesitate here. What is a person? I agree with Varela that if we are to find out, we shall require a new kind of science that takes contemplative practices such as meditation seriously. For two and a half thousand years, Buddhism has shown that consciousness doesn't depend upon an integrated, solid, "truly existing" self. Since the ecological thought appears to point this way, there may be a fruitful convergence somewhere down the line.

FORWARD PHILOSOPHY

There is a deeper problem for the hapless reactionaries we met at the beginning of this chapter—a problem for all of us, as a matter of fact. Pointing out the snow in your neighborhood suddenly becomes a mystifying, fetishistic operation in an era of global warming. Something seemingly real and cold and wet is less real, and pointing to it is less realistic, than something we can't directly sense. Reality as such has been upgraded so that phenomena you can see and hear and palpate have become less real than ones you can't. Reality seems to have a hole in it, like realizing that you're floating in outer space (which, of course, technically, we are). This affects our sense of orientation, which traditionally depended on a background of some kind, whether we called it Nature, lifeworld, or biology: whatever seems to lie beyond our ken, outside of our responsibility, or outside of the social. When there is no background, there is no foreground. This lack of a world is a real problem, a big problem—we have about five minutes for Schadenfreude as we watch the righties struggling with all this, and then we realize we are also spinning in the void. When there is no world, there is no ontology. What the hell is going on?

We can't nestle in a nice holistic burrow now that we've defeated the evil individualists. There is no burrow, therefore no nestling. So at the very same time as our world is really melting, our idea of what "really" and "real" mean also melts. The global warming crisis is also an opportunity to point that out, to notice that reality is a naked emperor.

There is global warming; there is an ecological emergency; I'm not a nihilist; the big picture view undermines right-wing ideology, which is why the right is so afraid of it. However, the melting world induces panic. This is a problem, philosophically and otherwise. Again, it's a paradox. While we absolutely have complete responsibility for global warming and must act now to curb emissions, we are also faced with various fantasies about "acting now," many of which are toxic to the kind of job humanists do. There is an ideological injunction to act "Now!" while humanists are tasked with slowing down, using our minds to find out what this all means.

There is a meme that theory is the opposite of practice. I've been accused of not wanting to help Katrina victims because I'm so busy theorizing with my head in the clouds: "Your ideas are all very well for a lazy Sunday afternoon, but out here in the real world, what are we actually going to do?" Yet one thing we must do is precisely break down the distinction between Sunday afternoon and every other day, and in the direction of putting a bit of Sunday afternoon into Monday morning, rather than making Sunday a workday.

The injunction to act now is ultimately based on preserving a Nature that we are finding out never existed. So the injunction has real effects that may result in more genuine catastrophe as we tilt at the nonexistent windmills of Nature. I'm definitely not saying, "Let's not look after animals because they're not really natural." I'm trying to find a reason to look after all beings on this planet precisely because they're not natural.

There have been a number of Copernican revolutions in human thinking about mind and society, revolutions that displaced human agency. Marx argued that the network of economic relationships underpinned the superstructure of beliefs and ideas. Freud showed that a field of unconscious processes structured conscious thinking. Saussure and, even more strongly, Derrida demonstrated that meaning took place within a structure that had strange properties independent of conscious intention. To this list we must add Darwin: a sprawling system of tiny, incremental differences in phenotypes, brought about through random DNA mutation, accounts for the existence of living organisms. We bear these massive "humiliations," these wounds to our narcissistic sense of importance.[64] It's the rigorous, structural quality of these Copernican ideas that the ecological thought must accept. The ecological thought has been trapped in a sticky web of "embedded and embodied" ideology—beliefs that we exist in a "lifeworld." These ideas impede—sometimes they even encourage us to feel proud about impeding—the big picture. Carriers of the lifeworld idea falsely hold rationality to be the problem, rather than the social forms in which reason emerged.

We can't go to the other extreme and take refuge in a transcendental mind. Imagining infinity might be easier, and more gratifying, than imagining very large finitudes such as 10^{84} cm^3—the volume of the Universe (according to Manfred Eigen).[65] Try this one: animals are a tiny finger of a small arm on a giant wheel of life forms mostly made up of bacteria and other single-celled forms.[66] The shock of very large finitude pertains to aesthetics: the awesome is easier than the truly disquieting. A blue whale is easier on the eye than a slime mold. Consider the political implications of climate disruption. What if it's not a huge catastrophe worthy of a Spielberg movie but a real drag, one that goes on for centuries? What if the disaster isn't an imminent cataclysm but has already occurred? What if this is how it looks? Humiliation rubs our face in *this* side of reality. There is no beyond, no depth, and no comforting background. No Being, only beings.[67]

The ecological thought will explore reductionism, the philosophy of "less than." It's not so much that we need to know exactly what a "person" is, but rather that we need to know exactly what a person isn't. It might be important to figure out whether persons really are solid, single, lasting, and independent beings. This has huge implications for ethics and politics. We need reasons for acting that aren't bound up with self-interest. Derek Parfit's extraordinarily prescient book *Reasons and Persons* (first published in 1984) begins to forge a non-self-interest-based ethics. Parfit demolishes the idea that persons are single, lasting, and independent. We need something like a "no-self" description of states of mind—"anger has arisen here" says enough of what is meaningful about "I am angry," without fixing emotions in the amber of identity.[68]

Selfishness may have no basis in the real. "Selfishness" only truly matters at the genomic level, where there isn't much of a self to go around.[69] We could argue that altruism, not selfishness, is hardwired into reality, since we are made of others: we've literally got them under our skin.[70] Darwin's idea of species resembles the Buddhist–Parfitian self: it exists, but not that much. Since we live in the mesh, because "we are the world" (that song has its uses), and because we are now conscious of ecological, evolutionary, and geological timescales, we must justify action by more than appeals to ourselves or to our immediate kin. Actions such as choosing to build, or not to build, a nuclear power station have consequences that can't be measured in consequentialist or utilitarian terms, because we have no idea how big the goalposts are.[71] Including big space and time, the ecological thought prevents us from establishing the size of the goalposts in advance. The future is one of those things like Nature, set up as a thing "over yonder": something else that the ecological thought dissolves. If there is no world, there is no future, since we can't assume a fixed temporal horizon, just as we can't assume a fixed spatial one. We can't throw empty cans into the ocean anymore and just pretend they have gone "away." Likewise, we can't kick the ecological can into the future and pretend it's gone "away."[72] There is a pc version of this pretense in some humanities' scholars insistence that non-Western people don't or can't (or even shouldn't) care about global warming, since they look to their own survival interests (perhaps down the road about two generations, but no more), and to their immediate phenomena, immersed as such scholars believe non-Western peasants to be in a rich lifeworld. The implication is that only certain privileged westerners care about global warming. This is nothing more than dangerously patronizing, assuming that non-Westerners can't hold more than one idea in mind at a time.

Evolution doesn't look ahead at all: as we've seen, DNA mutation is random with respect to current need. So we might as well admit that arguments based on utility are based on a teleology that the mesh just doesn't possess. The ecological thought compels us to recalibrate our sense of justice. And who precisely is doing the recalibrating? Problems with consequentialism imply problems with the notion of a (single, solid, independent) self. To believe in a self is actually to believe in an object, although it may seem a subtler kind of object than a brick or a chair. The no-self view is actually more "subjective," in a way. By not holding an objectlike picture of myself in mind, by being true to my inability to pin myself down, I'm being more honest. The ecological thought includes the subject, as our trip through dark ecology showed. The subject isn't an optional extra. Subjectivity is like a waterbed: push it down in one place, and it pops up in another. Thinking that personhood is the enemy of ecology is a big mistake. Unfortunately, it's fashionable to do so—another thing that joins postmodernists and deep ecologists. The ecological thought undermines metaphysics, whether your metaphysics says that there is one thing, or two things, or many things, or infinity things, or nothing.

Finding a progressive way to talk about population is one of Parfit's principal aims. William Godwin and Percy Shelley had a crack at a critique of Malthus in the early nineteenth century; their argument, frequently cited, is that Malthus deliberately ignores distributional inequities. Earth could support an awful lot of life forms if they all had enough to live on. Parfit, conversely, goes deeper. He exposes ideas based on self-interest theory, such as Malthusian population theory, to repeated prisoner's dilemma tests, which they fail. Along with radiation and pollution, population is one of the transpersonal, long-term, big picture things that we must now consider. A strong example of a more recent version of Malthusian self-interest theory is Garrett Hardin's infamous consequentialist "tragedy of the commons," which has had an inordinate effect on environmental thinking.

FORWARD ECONOMICS

Some crude economic ideologies oppose ecological progress, such as the facile neoliberal complaint that renewable energy would "hurt" the economy or that taxes on fuel are just lining the pockets of the government. Aren't all taxes doing this? Isn't that what a tax is? Some would prefer to put off carbon trading and solar power and await a perfect solution, like a toilet that teleported your waste into a black hole. We might have to wait an awfully long time for perfect recycling—it would require an ability to reverse entropy. This objection is related to the common psychological problem of not wanting to admit that there is a humiliating stain somewhere. Yet ecological ideologies often set limits. It seems absurdly churlish to question them. Who can deny the global food crisis, limits to the supply of gasoline, the general lack of enough to go around, the sense that the population is out of control?

Let's be churlish for a moment. A certain refusal to see the wood for the trees is built into capitalist ideology and reality. The division of labor means that people can't be as flexible as a testing ecological emergency requires. The system encourages the shock troops (such as truck drivers) to go on strike about rising oil prices and yell "Drill, baby, drill!" (the war cry of the 2008 Republican Convention). People keep playing zero sum games—looking after ecology means hurting the economy, and vice versa. Is it possible to fix this myopia within capitalism?

Capitalism ultimately can't sort things out. It's reactive; what we need is proactive. Consider hydrogen fuel: since fuel cells cost a lot of carbon to make, a sensible short-term solution would be to build a nuclear power plant to power a fuel cell factory (gulp). No corporation could do this spontaneously and alone, without social planning and choice. There is a bigger picture here. Since the so-called invisible hand of the market "decides" how to sort things out at the very moment at which it is ruining things, by the time the market "sorts it out," there will be nothing to sort out. Just as the two World Wars were appropriate disasters for the age of nationalism, so global warming is appropriate to the age of globalization. The two World Wars were nationalism run amok, something the system couldn't handle. Global warming is the symptom that global capitalism can't handle. The only solution is conscious cooperation. Far from aiding cooperation, ideological languages of passive immersion in Nature actually militate against it: either they support some version of laissez-faire, or they advertise regression to precapitalist social forms.

Perhaps the secret link between capitalism and scientism (scientific ideology, not science) is the weird sadistic distance implied in the almost experimental "Let the chips fall where they may" attitude—"Let it be" type artists beware. In Terry Gilliam's ecological apocalyptic time-loop movie, *Twelve Monkeys*, the lunatic who releases the virus that wipes out almost all humans doesn't even open the vial of deadly pathogens himself.[73] He allows an airport security officer to open it. The look on his face, the curious, fascinated "Hmm, I wonder what will happen if . . . ?" is horrifying. "Letting be" could be the message that makes someone press the button. I guess I prefer ecological noir to "let it be" art.

Gilliam's lunatic is obsessed with overpopulation. Malthus infests environmental ideology in various ways. By universally applying Malthus to all life forms, Darwin strangely canceled what was noxious about Malthus's work: that it was specifically designed to promote welfare cuts—an "is" used as a mighty "ought." Unlimited Malthusianism has no scary teeth: self interest only makes sense when there's a self distinct from others. But Hardin's idea of "the tragedy of the commons" grates on my left ecologist nerves. It's one of those things you hear people telling you to just accept as an inevitable part of reality. The "tragedy of the commons" is the idea that conflicting selfish interests will eventually deplete common property.[74] Hardin assumes that the "commons" is separate and autonomous: it "works by itself"; it replenishes itself. But that idea was already dead by the end of the eighteenth century. Hardin clearly never lived near any commons. There is only one way, and that is forward, which means talking about collective land, making conscious decisions, engineering, and so on. Ecology isn't about "resources," infinite or not. "Resources" is one of those ideas of something "over yonder" that the ecological thought deletes. Nor is there a counterfantasy of superabundance: this is defunct early capitalist language.[75]

What would you do if you were a prisoner who was given the choice of remaining silent or betraying another suspect, supposing the following to be the case?

1. If you both betray each other you will receive five years in jail.
2. If one of you betrays and the other is silent, the betrayed one will receive ten years in jail.
3. If you both remain silent, you will each get six months for a minor charge.

This is the prisoner's dilemma. The ecological thought is about considering others, in their interests, in how we should act toward them, and in their very being. Parfit helps us to transcend the "tragedy of the commons" view by allowing us to see how self-interest is at best indirectly self-defeating. Instead of lamenting an inevitable tragedy, we find ourselves having to make economic choices. Parfit imagines two future situations. In the first, there are many, many more humans than there are now, on the order of trillions, spread across many worlds. These people live close to a state of bliss. In the second, there are still more uncountable multitudes of people living on countless billions of worlds. These humans live close to what Parfit calls "the bad level," just above the level of sheer survival.[76] Even according to modified theories of self-interest that take others into account, the second model is preferable to the first one, because the mere existence of a human life is better than its nonexistence. See the problem? You could modify self-interest to include your family members, or all your descendants, or all of those plus their friends. However wide a circle you draw, you have to face the fact that, according to your theory, the bad level is better than utter bliss for several trillion sentient beings.

I'm not alone in thinking that consequentialism and hedonism won't do. John Vucetich and Michael Nelson argue that hoping for a better future is precisely what blocks ecological action. Vucetich and Nelson maintain that we should abandon hope (as they put it), if only because it's too easily hamstrung by that other environmentalist meme, the threat of imminent doom.[77] We should act ecologically out of a modified Kantian duty that doesn't depend on a powerful aesthetic experience such as the sublime to ground it. If it absolutely must depend on an experience, perhaps it should be a downgraded version that includes various experiences that Kant wants to edit out of the aesthetic, such as disgust—because the life forms whom we've got under our skin aren't something we can spit out. (*Ecology without Nature* argues that the trouble with the aesthetic dimension is that you can't just exit from it, rather like Alice trying to leave the Looking Glass House. Any postenvironmentalist ecological view must include the aesthetic.)[78] Perhaps the sentiment we're going for is not "We can because we must," but rather "We must because we are."

This means that we must base ecological action on ethics, not aesthetics. Ecological action will never feel good and the nonworld will never seem elegant. This is because we are not embedded in a lifeworld and can thus never get our bearings sufficiently to achieve the appropriate aesthetic distance from which to experience that kind of refined pleasure. Hedonistic forms of consequentialism—ideas, however expressed, that ecological concern makes us or others feel better—don't work. Environmental politics has been barking up the wrong tree, trying to make people feel or see something different. "If only we could see things differently" can be translated quickly into "I won't act unless suitably stimulated and soothed by a picture of reality built to my preexisting specifications." This is now impossible. We can't con ourselves into a touchy-feely reason to act.

This is beginning to look much more like Kantian ethics than the authoritarian voice of aesthetic compulsion. There is a twist, which is that Kantian duty gets its cue from a quasi-aesthetic experience that Kant calls sublimity, so we haven't totally edited the aesthetic out of the equation. We can't escape the experiential dimension of existence, and wouldn't be awful if we could? Yet the ecological thought drops Kantian aesthetics, too, if by that we mean being able to spit out disgusting things (the premise on which Kantian taste is built). We can't spit out the disgusting real of ecological enmeshment. It's just too close and too painful for comfort. So it's a weird, perverse aesthetics that includes the ugly and the horrifying, embracing the monster. Ultimately it means not swapping our dualism and our mechanism for something that seems nicer, such as vitalism or monism. We have to make do with the nasty stuff that has been handed to us on our plate. That includes the fact of consciousness, which forever puts me in a paradoxical relationship with other beings—there is always going to be an ironic gap between strange strangers. This is good news, actually, because it means I can be ecological without losing my sense of irony. Irony isn't just a slogan on a cool t-shirt; it's the way coexistence feels. Don't just do something—sit there. But in the mean time, sitting there will upgrade your version of doing and of sitting.

FORWARD POLITICS: STYLES OF COLLECTIVITY

This openness serves as an operating system for politics: it doesn't tell you what to do, exactly, but it opens your mind so you can think clearly about what to do. That we can actually use our minds to transcend our material conditions is the reason why the Kantian sublime is so utterly different from Edmund Burke's version. Burke's sublime is solid and awesome and powerful—there is no arguing with it; you just have to capitulate to it. His models are monarchy and mountains. There is too much of this kind of sublime in environmental aesthetics. This is why I just can't trust touchy-feeliness to think through the ecological emergency. It's seductive to imagine that a force bigger than global capitalism will finally sweep it away. But what if this thought were coming to us from within capitalism itself? What if capitalism itself relied on fantasies of apocalypse in order to keep reproducing and reinventing itself? What if, finally, Nature as such, the idea of a radical outside to the social system, was a capitalist fantasy, even precisely *the* capitalist fantasy?

Politics in the wake of the ecological thought must begin with the Copernican "humiliations"—coming closer to the actual dirt beneath our feet, the actuality of Earth. The ecological thought has no storyline. It is too much to throw up one's hands and say that life is cruel, like a character in a Thomas Hardy novel. Irony—economically expressed in the bumper sticker "You don't have to believe everything you think"—is perhaps the beginning of ecological democracy.[79] But irony doesn't necessarily mean detachment. Here are some affective states that we will encounter in pursuing the ecological thought: anger, compassion, confusion, curiosity, depression, disgust, doubt, grief, helplessness, honesty, humiliation, humility, openness, sadness, shame, and tenderness. None of these are necessarily incongruent with irony. In terms of how much they open us to the ecological thought, I'd rank compassion, curiosity, humility, openness, sadness, and tenderness the highest. Shame, which has been having a run for its money in recent philosophy, is still too dualistic to get things flowing.[80] Like the denouement in an M. Knight Shyamalan movie, inside the uncanny horror and fear is an almost unspeakable sadness. On the inside, true compassion might feel like helplessness. Yet it would consist in refraining from violence and aggression. Out goes authority and harmony. In comes cooperation and choice.

Evolution helps us see the properly ethical, philosophical, and political scope of animal rights. Animal rights may develop into questions of inter- and intraspecies cooperation. We already employ goats to mow lawns. Dolphins have harried fish toward the nets of West African fishermen so that they could share them. Pythagoreanism treated all living things as kindred.[81] Animals were put on trial in the Middle Ages.[82] But species don't exist. Amazingly, perhaps this fact means that evolution implies that we can make nonbiological choices. Fully accepting the ecological thought would be preparing oneself for true transcendence—true because one wouldn't be rejecting ecology.[83] Animals are not animals. Humans are not animals. Animals are not human. Humans are not human. DNA has no flavor. Nor is DNA a "blueprint" as the common prejudice believes—it's a set of algorithmic instructions, like a recipe book. There is no picture of me in my DNA. Our biological humanness consists in 0.1 percent of our genome: how in the world can we use this "is" to establish an "ought"?

According to this view, far from being classified as human, embryos could be classified as amoebae, since they share far more characteristics with them than with beings like mammals. Reductionism must be followed right the way through: then we can truly start building "ought"s without "is"s.[84] For example, the existence of universal cultural traits doesn't imply that they have a genetic basis.[85] If everything is biologically determined in some sense, then so is free will—then so what?[86] Since you can't base an "ought" on an "is," sociobiology can't base itself on, or make, moral or political judgments concerning society.

Some people have already tried modeling the complex kinds of democracy that take nonhuman beings into account.[87] A workable model will require some minimal (perhaps as minimal as possible) definition of collectivity.[88] Collective intimacy can't be about feeling part of something bigger or losing yourself in an intoxicating aesthetic rush: that way fascism lies.[89]

Ecological collectivity decisively can't be rooted in "place": as Levinas asserts, quoting Pascal, "my place in the sun" marks the beginning of all usurpation.[90] "Place" contains too much "at-homeness," too much finality, for the ecological thought. Localism, nationalism, and immersion in the ideological bath of the lifeworld, won't cut it anymore.[91] What we need is "a community without presuppositions and without subjects."[92] We need collectivity, not community. If this collectivity means not being part of something bigger, it must be a collectivity of weakness, vulnerability, and incompletion. Ecology without Nature is ecology without holism.

Ecological collectivity must think profoundly about choice: "history does nothing" (Marx).[93] Collectivity isn't just a whole bunch of "I"s, nor can it simply be a modified version of "alongsideness," of just happening to be next to one another.[94] Ecological collectivities must make space for introversion and reflection, including meditative practices. Ecological collectivities must be open, not closed totalities. They would involve "radical passivity."[95] If we take seriously the charge that the problem with science isn't the ideas it develops but the attitudes it sustains, then ecological society must work directly on attitudes. This means, ultimately, working on reflection, and this means meditation, if it's not just to involve replacing one set of objectified factoids with another. Meditation doesn't mean becoming "one with everything" or tuning in to (nonexistent) Nature—how could you? Meditation means exposing our conceptual fixations and exploring the openness of the mesh. Politics might begin to include (difficult word!) spirituality, in the sense of a radical questioning and opening: "losing oneself in things, losing oneself to the point of not being able to conceive of anything but things."[96] Meditation does not mean emptying the mind or suppressing the intellect. It doesn't mean doing nothing. Meditation will be part of nontheistic "spirituality" and politics.[97] Meditation implies an erotics of coexistence, not just letting things be.[98] Meditation is yoga, which means yoking: enacting or experiencing an intrinsic interconnectedness. This yoga doesn't have to do with yin–yang balance. It has to do with difference.

True cooperation must confront the necessity of forgiveness, beyond letting be. Letting things be includes "respect" and "tolerance," even "sympathy."[99] But we need something like the feminine warmth that Levinas describes as opening onto the infinite: gentleness, "a delightful lapse in being," not violence, opens the ecological thought.[100] According to this view, capitalist pleasure isn't bad because it is too enjoyable but because it isn't nearly pleasurable enough. This also goes for Chinese and Soviet Communism, with its ideology of "bourgeois comfort for all."[101] The ecological thought unfolds from this level of satisfaction. But this satisfaction is only a platform for further exploration.[102]

The ecological thought discovers different kinds of pleasure in feminine intimacy with the strange stranger.[103] Ecological collectivity welcomes nonhumans with tenderness. Levinas gives the evocative example of the nymphs and the faun in Debussy's ballet *The Afternoon of a Faun*. These strange strangers "manifest a soft warmth where being dissipates into radiance."[104] The caress of compassion is "infinitely mysterious."[105] Perhaps within the darkness we discovered in Chapter 2 is an even stranger, more delightfully disruptive warmth, to be approached with caresses of frailty and vulnerability.[106] This caress is "animal or infantile," a "passivity." Not being sure of what is happening, not being sure yet of who is who and what is what, this caress remains "in the *no man's land* between being and not-yet-being."[107] Biological fecundity provides a basis for imagining an infinite society.[108]

"Letting be" is just the flip side of laissez-faire ideology. There is something passive-aggressive in the injunction to leave things alone, withdrawing human "interference." There is something of the hunter in letting be: "Be vewy vewy quiet," as Elmer Fudd says, on the hunt for Bugs Bunny.[109] Yet I'm still responsible for the neighbor, even if she persecutes me. As the ice caps melt, perhaps we should be teaching drowning polar bears to use flotation devices. Perhaps we should be feeding the penguins until the seas contain enough fish. What needs to be removed is the barrier separating the beings we call cute (things in our garden, like pets) from the noncute (the Do Not Touch realm of Nature). "Letting be" is counter to the cute. There is a taste of scientistic coldness in it. The Earth is not an experiment. We can't just sit back and relax and let evolution do its thing. In this respect, deep ecology, which sees humans as a viral blip in the big Gaian picture, is nothing other than laissez-faire capitalism in a neofascist ideological form.

There is a pretty obvious reason why Republicans are in such denial about global warming. Accepting the truth of global warming would

mean that reality isn't wired for libertarianism or individualism or rigid
hierarchies or almost any of the other right-wing sacred cows. On the
global warming and global warming denial sites I visit all too regularly,
there are two major genres of statement. One is an injunction: "Well, global
warming is happening, but just let Nature/evolution take its course." This
implies that we have no responsibility for, nor should we feel any guilt
about, suffering beings and changing ecosystems. It also implies that
somehow there is an automated process going on (called Nature) that we
shouldn't interfere with—an invisible hand hardwired into reality "over
yonder" beyond our intentions, beyond society (which is itself modeled, in
this view, as a social contract between freely agreeing individuals). The
other genre of statement is a denial of totality: "Well, it snowed in Boise,
Idaho, last week, so it's not warming up where I am, so global warming is
a crock of . . ." (These arguments are easily refuted, as I did at the start of
this chapter.)

Observe that these two genres suffer from Freud's borrowed kettle syndrome: there are too many reasons to deny global warming, reasons that
contradict each other.[110] Global warming is happening, and we should just
let Nature take its course; global warming isn't happening, so stop whin-
ing about it. There is a third statement genre, actually, something like:
"Okay, it's happening, but there's no proof that we caused it" (the reactionaries' favorite phrase is "anthropogenic global warming," which makes
it sound scary and geeky). I suppose this genre is somewhere in between
denial and acceptance.

What can we learn from these genres of global warming denial? Perhaps the first is that the perceived threat is (and here I'm going to sound
like Oscar Wilde) far more than merely real—it's also a fantasmic threat,
that is, a threat to reactionary fantasy as such. To accept global warming
is to give up your fantasy that we are individuals who have just agreed on
a level playing field to have a social contract; that capitalism is an automated process that must continue without intervention of even a mildly
social-democratic kind. These two halves of reactionary sentiment are
already intrinsically at odds with one another—one is about agreements
freely chosen; another is about an automated process you have to leave
alone. The global warming view, from the reactionary standpoint, involves inverting both halves of the sentiment. Society is not an agreement

between presocial individuals but an already existing totality for which we are directly responsible.

Capitalism is a boiling whirlwind of impermanence. It reveals how things are always shifting and changing. But it isn't the ultimate horizon of meaning. Capitalism does have structure—the relationship between owners and workers, for instance. It has predictability, patterns in the chaos. And, curiously, capitalism creates things that are more solid than things ever were. Alongside global warming, "hyperobjects" will be our lasting legacy. Materials from humble Styrofoam to terrifying plutonium will far outlast current social and biological forms. We are talking about hundreds and thousands of years. Five hundred years from now, polystyrene objects such as cups and takeout boxes will still exist. Ten thousand years ago, Stonehenge didn't exist. Ten thousand years from now, plutonium will still exist.

Hyperobjects do not rot in our lifetimes. They do not burn without themselves burning (releasing radiation, dioxins, and so on). The ecological thought must think the future of these objects, these toxic things that appear almost more real than reality itself, like the acidic blood of the Alien in Ridley Scott's film, which burns through metal floors.[111] This blood is a science fiction version of demonic ichor.[112] Reason must find a way to deal with these demonic substances. With its apocalyptic visions and thousand-year itches, Christianity isn't ready for hyperobjects. Yet, thinking about these materials does involve something like religion, because they transcend our personal death. Living tissue is usually far more stable than chemical compounds. But hyperobjects outlast us all.

There is a joke about wanting to be reborn as a Styrofoam cup—they last forever. Hyperobjects don't just burn a hole in the world; they burn a hole in your mind. Plutonium is truly astonishing to contemplate. We think of light as neutral or benign. Radiation is poisoned light. We think of "objects" as passive and inert, as "over there." Just by existing, this hyperobject affects living tissue. Radioactive materials are already "over here," inside our skin, as Marie Curie discovered to her cost. Driving past Rocky Flats, the decommissioned nuclear bomb trigger factory near Boulder, Colorado, is frightening and disorienting. Did I inhale a speck of plutonium on my way to visit my family? Hyperobjects invoke a terror beyond the sublime, cutting deeper than conventional religious fear. A massive cathedral dome, the mystery of a stone circle, have nothing on the sheer existence of hyperobjects.

Humans have manufactured materials that are already beyond the normal scope of our comprehension. As I argued earlier, we need justifications for our actions that go beyond bankrupt and downright dangerous self-interest theories. Climate change—the result of about two hundred years of human industry—could change Earth for thousands of years. Plutonium will be around for far longer than all of recorded human "history" so far. If you want a monument, look around you.

There is a way to spin this. A good example would be the ideological force of the so-called butterfly effect—the idea based on mathematical Chaos theory that a butterfly flapping its wings in Brazil could set off a tornado in Texas.[113] Ideologies are commands pretending to be descriptions. In this case, the statement enjoins us to think and act small. Related is the popular systems theory idea of "emergence," that systems can organize themselves without much (or any) conscious input.[114] The ideology is expressed in the "hundredth monkey principle"—once you persuade a hundred monkeys to do something, the whole tribe will do it. Even if this is true, how do you persuade the ninetieth monkey? The eightieth?

The ideology of emergence states that we don't need to take responsibility for good decisions—they will just happen "naturally." But to tackle pollution, climate disruption, and radiation, we must think and act big, which means thinking and acting collectively. This will take conscious input. We will have to choose to act and think together. We won't be able to stumble upon the right solutions. Society isn't like a bunch of molecules randomly jostling each other with Brownian motion. As Darwin argued, even butterflies value choice.[115] It's one of the abiding curiosities of capitalist ideology that it accords a gigantic value to choice in one sense, and none whatsoever in another.

Suppose that future humans achieve a society that is less materialistic than ours. This will probably be the case, if only to prevent human extinction. They will be less materialistic, but the actually existing products of profound materialism will persist, haunting them like inverse ghosts: more solid than solid, more real than real, "nearer than breathing, closer than hands and feet."[116] Is it not impossible that future humans will have built something like spirituality around these materials?[117] Care for the hyperobject will emerge. Return for a moment to the question of the nuclear power plant powering the fuel cell factory. What do you do with the radioactive waste? You can't just sweep it under the Yucca Mountain carpet and hope nobody notices. You know too much—we live in Ulrich Beck's risk society. So you have to store it, ideally above ground in monitored retrievable storage, for thousands of years. Hyperobjects are the true taboos, the demonic inversion of the sacred substances of religion. The recent plan to dispose of nuclear materials by putting small amounts in regular household silverware was perhaps the most outrageous "solution" yet.[118] Future humans' treatment of hyperobjects may seem like reverence to our eyes. Isn't it ironic that supposedly materialist, secular societies created the ultimate spiritual substances? This is truly a case of the chickens coming home to roost. With all due respect to Jacques Lacan, what to do with their poop will be the last thing on future humans' (or humanoids') minds.

We become aware of the worldness of the world only in a globalizing environment in which fiber optic cables run under the ocean and satellites hover above the ionosphere. There was no world before capitalism. This sounds shocking to some environmentalists, but the ecological thought is indeed shocking. We are becoming aware of the world at the precise moment at which we are "destroying" it—or at any rate, globally reshaping it. Nature appears in a world of industrial, privatized farming. Marx put it in his inimitably ruthless way: "First the labourers are driven from the land, and then the sheep arrive."[119] He forgot to add: and then Nature shows up. Things are first known when lost, as Edward Thomas wrote:

> I never had noticed it until
> 'Twas gone,—the narrow copse
> Where now the woodman lops
> The last of the willows with his bill
>
> It was not more than a hedge overgrown.
> One meadow's breadth away
> I passed it day by day.
> Now the soil is bare as bone.   (1–8)[120]

Nature as such appears when we lose it, and it's known as loss. Along with the disorientation of the modern world goes an ineffable sadness. Writing during the First World War, Thomas knew how globally disruptive events drastically change our physical and mental landscape. The First World War was a horrifying combination of modern technology and old school battle strategy, and a glimpse at Paul Nash's painting *We Are Building a New World* (1918) will convince you of the environmental vision of artists at this time. Ecological disaster is a warlike experience—the Pentagon is concerned about the political consequences of climate disruption.[121] The total destruction of nuclear war is upon us, in an ultra-slow-motion version. We look around and see what we are losing as a "thing" that is disappearing from our grasp and out from under our feet.

Two things that seem distinct—human society and Nature—are two different angles of the same thing. As far as location and cohabiting go, feudal peasants had no choice: neither did slaves, nor did indigenous peoples. Now we have the first stirrings of a choice: are we going to choose, and how? This is very different from saying that capitalism is the be-all and end-all of existence. Since its beginnings, capitalism has used war and catastrophe to reinvent itself. The current catastrophe is no exception. We should reject the false choice between the "politics of possibility" and a "return to nature." Instead, let's use this moment to imagine what sort of noncapitalist society we want.

We have reached not the end of history, as Francis Fukuyama would have it, but only the beginning.[122] We have barely become conscious that we have been terraforming Earth all along. Now we have the chance to face up to this fact and to our coexistence with all beings. Freud compares psychoanalysis to reclamation work: "a work of culture, like the draining of the Zuider Zee."[123] Psychoanalysis is terraforming. Terraforming is psychoanalysis—bringing things to consciousness, owning up to our consciousness and our choices. Sorry to say, we have lost soft, squishy, irrational, authoritarian Nature. We have really lost it, because it never even existed. We have lost even the idea of it. Losing a fantasy is harder than losing a reality—just ask a therapist. Consciousness sucks. The more you're aware of ecology, the more you lose the very "world" you were trying to save and the more things you didn't know or didn't want to know come to the fore. The room for acting out shrinks. But this realization also means that there is an ecological life after capitalism. Capitalism doesn't exhaust every potential of ecological politics and ethics.

While their assertion of "the death of environmentalism" resembles my phrase "ecology without Nature," Ted Nordhaus and Michael Shellenberger are wrong. It's no surprise that their book *Break Through* employs Fukuyama in full ideological mode: capitalism is the end of history—get used to it. *Break Through*'s subtitle is *From the Death of Environmentalism to the Politics of Possibility*.[124] "Possibility" is nicely poised between potentiality and inevitability. Make do with what you're given. Nordhaus and Shellenbereger advocate not so much a "politics of possibility" but the usual miserable oppressiveness of the capitalist reality principle. Their argument superficially resembles mine: they claim, for instance, that a reified product called "the environment" is getting in the way of meaningful ecological politics. But Nordhaus and Schellenberger rely on limiting our scope to a narrow chink in a preexisting prison window, reducing ecological thinking to realpolitik. The injunction to get on with it and put up with the social conditions we have can easily become another brick in the prison wall that inhibits the possibility of escape. To this end, the rhetoric of sustainability becomes a weapon in the hands of global corporations that would like nothing better than to reproduce themselves in perpetuity. The current social situation becomes a thing of Nature, a tree that you're preserving—a plastic object you must maintain on pain of death. This social situation is at the same time totally autonomous from you yourself, the actual you—it's an "emergent" feature like a wave that doesn't concern you as a mere droplet of water. We are back to our poor old Republican deniers and their contradictory mindset.

Far from rubbishing deep ecology as a religious objectification, we should take its claims more seriously than it takes them, and go even deeper, deeper into the mesh. We are only just beginning to think the ecological thought. Perhaps there is no end to its thinking. T. S. Eliot declared, "Human kind / Cannot bear very much reality" (*Burnt Norton*, lines 44–45).[125] We must do far more than bear it. There might be seeds of future ways of being together in religion, as there are in art. Perhaps the new eco-religions offer hints of postcapitalist coexistence. This coexistence is almost unimaginable, so it appears as religion. The ecological thought must conceive of postcapitalist pleasures, not bourgeois pleasure for the masses but forms of new, broader, more rational pleasure; not boring, overstimulating bourgeois reality, not fridges and cars and anorexia for all, but a world of being, not having, as Erich Fromm puts it. It must guard against ideologies of social regression—the "return to Nature" in its frightening guises. One always proposes returning to Nature from a certain position in the here and now, so that calls to go back can't help being exercises in bad faith.[126] Yet historical change may feel like taking steps backward. Capitalism has so co-opted the idea of "progress" that anything else, as one philosopher said, might feel like yanking on the emergency brake.[127]

Religion is a substitute for lost intimacy.[128] If Nature is religion, then the intimacy it expresses as lost returns in ecology's encounter with the strange stranger. The ecological thought successfully mourns for a Nature that never really existed anyway, except in some ideological pipe dream. But it isn't completely "over" religion. If reason has no place for intimacy, the ecological thought will indeed seem religious. If the void opened up by the mesh seems too profound, we might be tempted to freeze it into religion.

How to care for the neighbor, the strange stranger, and the hyperobject, are the long-term problems posed by the ecological thought. The ecological thought hugely expands our ideas of space and time. It forces us to invent ways of being together that don't depend on self-interest. After all, other beings elicited the ecological thought: they summon it from us and force us to confront it. They compel us to imagine collectivity rather than community—groups formed by choice rather than by necessity. Strange strangers and hyperobjects goad us to greater levels of consciousness, which means more stress, more disappointment, less gratification (though perhaps more satisfaction), and more bewilderment. The ecological thought can be highly unpleasant. But once you have started to think it, you can't unthink it. We have started to think it. In the future, we will all be thinking the ecological thought. It's irresistible, like true love.

Notes

ABBREVIATIONS

AT   Richard Dawkins, *The Ancestor's Tale: A Pilgrimage to the Dawn of Life* (London: Phoenix, 2005).

DDI   Daniel C. Dennett, *Darwin's Dangerous Idea: Evolution and the Meanings of Life* (New York: Simon & Schuster, 1995).

DM   Charles Darwin, *The Descent of Man, and Selection in Relation to Sex*, intro. by James Moore and Adrian Desmond (Harmondsworth: Penguin, 2004).

EP   Richard Dawkins, *The Extended Phenotype: The Long Reach of the Gene* (Oxford: Oxford University Press, 1999).

EwN   Timothy Morton, *Ecology without Nature: Rethinking Environmental Aesthetics* (Cambridge, MA: Harvard University Press, 2007).

OB   Emmanuel Levinas, *Otherwise Than Being: or, Beyond Essence*, trans. Alphonso Lingis (Pittsburgh: Duquesne University Press, 1998).

OED   *Oxford English Dictionary*, online edition, dictionary.oed.com.

OS   Charles Darwin, *The Origin of Species*, ed. Gillian Beer (Oxford: Oxford University Press, 1996).

PAI   Margaret A. Boden, ed., *The Philosophy of Artificial Intelligence* (Oxford: Oxford University Press, 1990).

TI   Emmanuel Levinas, *Totality and Infinity: An Essay on Exteriority*, trans. Alphonso Lingis (Pittsburgh: Duquesne University Press, 1969).

INTRODUCTION: CRITICAL THINKING

1. Percy Shelley, *A Defence of Poetry*, in *Shelley's Poetry and Prose*, ed. Donald H. Reiman and Neil Fraistat (New York: Norton, 2002), 530.

2. For example, see the Church of Deep Ecology: churchofdeepecology.org.

3. Andrew Stanton, dir., *Wall • E* (Pixar Animation Studios, 2008).

4. Shelley, *A Defence of Poetry*, 535.

5. *OS*, 248–251.

6. *TI*, 25.

7. *EwN*, 204–205.

8. Alexander Pope, *Essay on Man* 1.294, in *The Poems of Alexander Pope: A One-Volume Edition of the Twickenham Text, with Selected Annotations*, ed. John Butt (London: Routledge, 1989).

9. Paul McCartney (and Martin Heidegger), "Let It Be," *Let It Be* (Apple Records, 1970).

10. John Donne, *Meditation 17*, in *Major Works: Including Songs and Sonnets and Sermons*, ed. John Carey (Oxford: Oxford University Press, 2000), 344.

11. See *EwN*, 14, 18–19, 83–92.

12. See Steven Vogel, *Against Nature: The Concept of Nature in Critical Theory* (Albany: State University of New York Press, 1996).

13. John Barrell, *The Idea of Landscape and the Sense of Place, 1730–1840: An Approach to the Poetry of John Clare* (Cambridge: Cambridge University Press, 1972); and *The Dark Side of the Landscape: The Rural Poor in English Painting, 1730–1840* (Cambridge: Cambridge University Press, 1980).

14. *EwN*, 20–21, 22, 52–53, 67, 80–81, 105–106, 114–115, 142, 155, 168. In refraining from using "web" I'm trying to follow my own rules, though "mesh" may be a poor substitute (see *EwN*, 81).

15. Pall Skulason, *Reflections at the Edge of Askja: On Man's Relation to Nature* (Reykjavik: University of Iceland Press, 2006), 11. See Slavoj Žižek, *In Defense of Lost Causes* (London: Verso, 2008), 444.

16. *TI*, 46.

17. René Descartes, *Meditations and Other Metaphysical Writings*, trans. with an intro. by Desmond M. Clarke (London: Penguin, 2000), 19.

18. *EwN*, 4–5, 63–64, 80–81, 124–125, 129, 128–135, 164, 168.

19. I borrow "restrictive economy" from Georges Bataille, *The Accursed Share: An Essay on General Economy*, trans. Robert Hurley (New York: Zone Books, 1988), 1:19–26 (25).

20. The "cyborg" represents personhood in an age of digital and ecological interconnectedness: see Donna Haraway, "A Cyborg Manifesto: Science, Technology, and Socialist-Feminism in the Late Twentieth Century," in *Simians, Cyborgs, and Women: The Reinvention of Nature* (London: Routledge, 1991), 149–181.

21. See, for example, Timothy Morton, "John Clare and the Question of Place," in *Romanticism's Debatable Lands*, ed. Claire Lamont and Michael Rossington (London: Palgrave, 2007), 105–117.

22. See Erich Fromm, *To Have or to Be?* (London: Continuum, 2007), 75.

23. See Elizabeth Royte, "A Tall, Cool Drink of . . . Sewage?" *New York Times Magazine*, August 10, 2008, 30–33.

24. Ryan Parker, "Residents Upset about Park Proposal," *Lakewood Sentinel*, July 31, 2008, milehighnews.com/Articles-i-2008-07-31-207468.114125_Residents_upset_about_park_proposal.html; "Solar Foes Focus in the Dark," Edito-

rial, August 7, 2008, milehighnews.com/Articles-i-2008–08–07–207541.114125_
Solar_foes_focus_in_the_dark.html; and August 14, 2008, 1, 4.

25. See, for example, Lawrence Buell, *The Environmental Imagination: Thoreau, Nature Writing, and the Formation of American Culture* (Cambridge, MA: Harvard University Press, 1995); Jonathan Bate, *Romantic Ecology: Wordsworth and the Environmental Tradition* (London: Routledge, 1991); Bate, *The Song of the Earth* (Cambridge, MA: Harvard University Press, 2000); James McKusick, *Green Writing: Romanticism and Ecology* (New York: St. Martin's Press, 2000); and Karl Kroeber, *Ecological Literary Criticism: Romantic Imagining and the Biology of Mind* (New York: Columbia University Press, 1994). See also Greg Garrard, *Ecocriticism* (London: Routledge, 2004); Kevin Hutchings, *Imagining Nature: Blake's Environmental Poetics* (Montreal: McGill-Queen's University Press, 2003); Ralph Pite, "How Green Were the Romantics?" *Studies in Romanticism* 35, no. 3 (Spring 1996): 357–373; Kate Rigby, *Topographies of the Sacred: The Poetics of Place in British Romanticism* (Charlottesville: University of Virginia Press, 2004); Onno Oerlemans, *Romanticism and the Materiality of Nature* (Toronto: University of Toronto Press, 2002).

26. See *EwN*, 73–76, 194–195.

27. For the analysis of environmental form, see Timothy Morton, "Of Matter and Meter: Environmental Form in Coleridge's 'Effusion 35' and 'The Eolian Harp,'" *Literature Compass Romanticism* 5 (January 2008), blackwell-compass.com/subject/literature/section_home?section=lico-romanticism.

28. *DDI*, 115, n. 10.

29. The word sometimes used is "continuism," from Jacques Derrida, *The Animal That Therefore I Am*, ed. Marie-Louise Mallet, trans. David Wills (New York: Fordham University Press, 2008), 30. The assumption that Derrida always knows what he is talking about is not Derridean. Derrida is also responsible for "asinane" (18, 31). Derrida finds himself in company with Luc Ferry, "Neither Man nor Stone," in Peter Atterton and Matthew Calarco, eds., *Animal Philosophy: Ethics and Identity* (London: Continuum, 2007), 147–156 (155). For a different view, see Felipe Fernández-Armesto, *So You Think You're Human? A Brief History of Humankind* (Oxford: Oxford University Press, 2004), 37.

30. Peter Atterton, "Ethical Cynicism," in Atterton and Calarco, eds., *Animal Philosophy*, 51–61 (61). Gilles Deleuze and Félix Guattari assert that they are beyond evolution in proposing the codevelopment of all beings in "alliance": "Becoming-Animal," in Atterton and Calarco, eds., *Animal Philosophy*, 87–100 (88). On the contrary, symbiosis, far from being the opposite of evolution, is deeply entrenched in it.

31. Jacques Derrida, *Of Grammatology*, trans. Gayatri Chakravorty Spivak (Baltimore: Johns Hopkins University Press, 1987), 162.

32. William Blake, *The Complete Poetry and Prose of William Blake*, ed. D. V. Erdman (New York: Doubleday, 1988), 667.

33. By "attitude" I mean what Lacanian ideology theory calls "subject position."

34. See, for instance, Slavoj Žižek, "Ecology without Nature," talk given at Panteion University, Athens, youtube.com/watch?v=CTYrCbDeut8&feature=related.

35. Timothy Morton, "Queer Ecology," *PMLA* (2010) (forthcoming); "Thinking Ecology: The Mesh and the Strange Stranger," *Collapse* 6 (2010), 265–293; "Ecologocentrism: Unworking Animals," *SubStance* 37, no. 3 (2008): 37–61.

36. Timothy Morton, "Of Matter and Meter," "John Clare and the Question of Place," and "Shelley, Nature and Culture," in *The Cambridge Companion to Shelley*, ed. Timothy Morton (Cambridge: Cambridge University Press, 2006), 185–207; "Wordsworth Digs the Lawn," *European Romantic Review* 15, no. 2 (March 2004): 317–327; "Why Ambient Poetics?" *The Wordsworth Circle* 33, no. 1 (Winter 2002): 52–56.

37. Richard Karban and Mikaela Huntzinger, *How to Do Ecology: A Concise Handbook* (Princeton, NJ: Princeton University Press, 2006), 46.

38. See Barbara Maria Stafford, *Voyage into Substance: Art, Science, Nature, and the Illustrated Travel Account, 1760–1840* (Cambridge, MA: MIT Press, 1984), 369.

39. I develop the concept of the strange stranger from Derrida's *arrivant*, the ultimate arrival to whom one must extend ultimate hospitality. Jacques Derrida, "Hostipitality," in *Acts of Religion*, ed., trans., and intro. by Gil Anidjar (London: Routledge, 2002), 356–420.

40. Harve Foster and Wilfred Jackson, dirs., *Song of the South* (Disney, 1946).

41. Ross Robertson, "A Brighter Shade of Green: Rebooting Environmentalism for the 21st Century," *What Is Enlightenment?* 38 (2008), wie.org/j38/bright-green .asp?page=3.

42. Coastlines have a fractal geometry. See James Gleick, *Chaos: Making a New Science* (Harmondsworth: Penguin, 1988) 84–89.

43. *OS*, 395–396.

1. THINKING BIG

1. E. F. Schumacher, *Small Is Beautiful: Economics as if People Mattered* (New York: Harper & Row, 1973); Frances Moore Lappé, *Diet for a Small Planet* (New York: Ballantine Books, 1971). Vegetarianism may become more necessary as human needs outstrip our capacity to feed livestock.

2. See Robert Kaufman, "Red Kant, or the Persistence of the Third *Critique* in Adorno and Jameson," *Critical Inquiry* 26 (Summer 2000): 682–724.

3. John Milton, *Paradise Lost*, ed. John Leonard (Harmondsworth: Penguin, 2003).

4. See *TI*, 197–198.

5. See Christof Koch, *The Quest for Consciousness: A Neurobiological Approach* (Englewood, CO: Roberts, 2004), 33, 35, 83–84, 140–144, 250–255, 264–268.

6. *TI*, 62.

7. Milton, Preface, *Paradise Lost*, 1.

8. Percy Bysshe Shelley, *The Poems of Shelley*, ed. Kelvin Everest and Geoffrey Matthews, 3 vols. (London: Longman, 1989–).

9. Roman Kroitor and Colin Low, *Universe* (National Film Board of Canada, 1960); Carl Sagan, *Contact: A Novel* (New York: Simon and Schuster, 1985); Robert Zemeckis, dir., *Contact* (Warner Brothers, 1997).

10. See Ursula K. Heise, *Sense of Place and Sense of Planet* (Oxford: Oxford University Press, 2008).

11. See Elizabeth Mitchell, "Cows Shown to Align North-South," *BBC News*, August 25, 2008, news.bbc.co.uk/1/hi/sci/tech/7575459.stm. Heise discusses how John Klima's installation *Earth* is a "database art" that works with forms of global knowledge in an environmental era (*Sense of Place and Sense of Planet*, 65–67).

12. Ulrich Beck, *Risk Society: Towards a New Modernity*, trans. Mark Ritter (London: Sage, 1992). See Heise, *Sense of Place and Sense of Planet*, 146–151, 154–159.

13. Tulku Urgyen Rinpoche, *As It Is* (Boudhanath: Rangjung Yeshe, 1999), 103–104.

14. See Rebecca French, *The Golden Yoke: The Legal Cosmology of Buddhist Tibet* (Ithaca, NY: Cornell University Press, 1995).

15. Martin Heidegger, "Being Dwelling Thinking," in *Poetry, Language, Thought*, trans. Albert Hofstadter (New York: Harper & Row, 1971), 141–160.

16. Spiritualized, *Ladies and Gentlemen We Are Floating in Space* (Arista, 1997).

17. *Today*, BBC Radio 4, May 6, 2008.

18. *OED*, "mesh," n.1.a–c.

19. *OED*, "mesh," n.2.

20. *OS*, 105–106.

21. *OS*, 107.

22. *OS*, 100, 141.

23. *OS*, 68, 79.

24. *OS*, 161.

25. William Wordsworth, "Prospectus to *Home at Grasmere*," 1002–1011, in *The Major Works: Including the Prelude*, ed. Stephen Gill (Oxford: Oxford University Press, 2008), 198.

26. William Blake, *The Complete Poetry and Prose of William Blake*, ed. D. V. Erdman (New York: Doubleday, 1988), 667.

27. *OS*, 151.

28. *EP*, 179–180 (and 179–194 in general).

29. See Stephen Jay Gould, *Wonderful Life: The Burgess Shale and the Nature of History* (New York: Norton, 1989). See *OS*, 67, 69, 70, 79.

30. *OS*, 62–63.

31. narsad.org/news/newsletter/profiles/profile2003–06–25c.html.

32. Roland Emmerich, dir., *The Day after Tomorrow* (20th Century Fox, 2004).

33. H. P. Lovecraft, "Through the Gates of the Silver Key," in *The Dream-Quest of Unknown Kadath* (New York: Ballantine Books, 1970), 191–192.

34. See Slavoj Žižek, *Looking Awry: An Introduction to Jacques Lacan through Popular Culture* (Cambridge, MA: MIT Press, 1991), 35–39; *In Defense of Lost Causes* (London: Verso, 2008), 420–461.

35. See, for example, Erich Fromm, *To Have or to Be?* (London: Continuum, 2007), 140.

36. "How He Did It," *Newsweek*, November 17, 2008, 41, 44, newsweek.com/id/167582/page/2.

37. Jacques Lacan, address given at MIT, quoted in Sherry Turkle, *Psychoanalytic Politics: Freud's French Revolution* (New York: Basic Books, 1978), 238. As Darwin observes, animals such as dogs and cats have developed behaviors for burying excrements: Charles Darwin, *The Expression of the Emotions in Man and Animals*, intro., afterword, and commentary by Paul Erkman (London: Harper Collins, 1999), 50, 51–52. Darwin remarks that dogs retain this habit from a remote common ancestor (50). Doesn't this make canine disposal at least as interesting as human disposal? Besides, if Lacan based his remark on settled agricultural societies (rather than, say, nomadic ones), then the "problem" isn't general to humankind.

38. Richard Scarry, *Busy, Busy, Town* (New York: Golden Books, 2000), 17.

39. See Timothy Clark, "Towards a Deconstructive Environmental Criticism," *Oxford Literary Review* 30, no. 1 (2008), 45–68 (48–52).

40. Theodor Adorno: "there is [a universal history] leading from the slingshot to the megaton bomb," *Negative Dialectics*, trans. E. B. Ashton (New York: Continuum, 1973), 320.

41. Henry David Thoreau, *The Maine Woods* (Harmondsworth: Penguin, 1988), 95.

42. *EP*, 159.

43. *AT*, 490, 500–501, 504, 513–514, 515, 517, 543–544, 546–548, 550–551.

44. *EP*, 178.

45. This is an inversion of Deleuze and Guattari's "body without organs," an image of the mind. See *EP*, 159; Gilles Deleuze and Félix Guattari, *Anti-Oedipus: Capitalism and Schizophrenia*, trans. Robert Hurley, Mark Seem, and H. Lane (Minneapolis: University of Minnesota Press, 1983), 1–8. Both Lynn Margulis and Slavoj Žižek have used the Cheshire cat's grin to similar effect: see *EP*, 223; Slavoj Žižek, *Organs without Bodies: Deleuze and Consequences* (New York: Routledge, 2003).

46. Richard Karban and Mikaela Huntzinger, *How to Do Ecology: A Concise Handbook* (Princeton, NJ: Princeton University Press, 2006), 39.

47. *EP*, 200–223, 226.

48. Mark T. Boyd, Christopher M. R. Bax, Bridget E. Bax, David L. Bloxam, and Robin A. Weiss, "The Human Endogenous Retrovirus ERV-3 Is Upregulated in Differentiating Placental Trophoblast Cells," *Virology* 196 (1993): 905–909.

49. K. W. Jeon and J. F. Danielli, "Micrurgical Studies with Large Free-Living Amebas," *International Reviews of Cytology*, 30 (1971): 49–89, quoted in *EP*, 160.

50. *EP*, 234–239, 239.

51. *AT*, 216–218.

52. See *AT*, 375.

53. See *EP*, 159. This fact has major implications. For example, systems theory explains living organisms as distinguishing an inside from an outside. The

inside–outside distinction founds metaphysical systems. See Jacques Derrida, "Violence and Metaphysics," in *Writing and Difference*, trans. Alan Bass (London: Routledge and Kegan Paul, 1978), 79–153 (151–152); "Plato's Pharmacy," in *Dissemination*, trans. Barbara Johnson (Chicago: University of Chicago Press, 1981), 63–171.

54. For a study of the philosophical and cultural implications of nanoscale objects, see Colin Milburn, *Nanovision: Engineering the Future* (Durham, NC: Duke University Press, 2008).

55. Eduardo Kac, *GFP Bunny* (2000), ekac.org/gfpbunny.html.

56. Malthus's *Essay on the Principles of Population* influenced both Darwin and Alfred Russel Wallace's theories of evolution. But does this mean Darwin himself was a "social Darwinist"? See *DDI*, 393, 461–463.

57. See Mary Midgley, *Evolution as a Religion* (London: Routledge, 2002).

58. Karl Marx, *Capital*, trans. Ben Fowkes (Harmondsworth: Penguin, 1990), 1.638.

59. In particular, see George Miller, dir., *Happy Feet* (Kingdom Feature Productions, 2006).

60. Sesame Street, "We Are All Earthlings," *Sesame Street Platinum All-Time Favorites* (Sony, 1995).

61. *OS*, 64.

62. Lynn Margulis, *Symbiosis in Cell Evolution* (San Francisco: Freeman, 1979); Lynn Margulis and Dorion Sagan, *Microcosmos* (New York: Simon & Schuster, 1986).

63. Derrida, "Violence and Metaphysics," 151–152.

64. I am using structuralist terminology derived from Ferdinand De Saussure's *System of General Linguistics*, ed. Charles Bally and Albert Sechehaye, trans. Roy Harris (London: Duckworth, 1983).

65. Yongey Mingyur Rinpoche, *The Joy of Living: Unlocking the Secret of Science and Happiness* (New York: Harmony Books, 2007), 174–175.

66. The classic instance is Jean-Paul Sartre, *Critique of Dialectical Reason*, 2 vols. (New York: Verso, 2009).

67. See Douglas Hofstadter, *Gödel, Escher, Bach: An Eternal Golden Braid* (New York: Basic Books, 1999), 222–223.

68. See *TI*, 137, 274.

69. *TI*, 173.

70. *TI*, 292, 294, 298, 302, 305.

71. Quoted in Slavoj Žižek, *For They Know Not What They Do: Enjoyment as a Political Factor* (London: Verso, 1994), 124.

72. The "strange stranger" is my translation of Jacques Derrida's *arrivant*. "Hostipitality," in *Acts of Religion*, ed., trans., and intro. by Gil Anidjar (London: Routledge, 2002), 356–420.

73. Emmanuel Levinas argues that the reality of Being is "strangeness": see *Existence and Existents*, trans. Alphonso Lingis, foreword by Robert Bernasconi (Pittsburgh: Duquesne University Press, 1988), 9.

74. *OS*, 106.

75. Donald Rumsfeld, Defense Department Briefing, February 12, 2002, defenselink.mil/transcripts/transcript.aspx?transcriptid=2636.

76. *OB*, 93; see *TI*, 24, 39, 40, 50–51, 75, 187–193, 197–201; "Interview," in *Animal Philosophy: Ethics and Identity*, ed. Peter Atterton and Matthew Calarco (London: Continuum, 2007), 49–50; *OB*, 12–13, 49, 69, 87–88. On several occasions, Levinas leaves the door open for nonhuman beings, explicitly or implicitly (for instance, in explorations of the caress and of carnality): *TI*, 156, 199, 213–214, 256–259, 270, 272, 276–277.

77. Mary Anning (1799–1847) discovered the skeleton of an ichthyosaur at Lyme Regis, Dorset, England, in 1811.

78. "Natural beauty, purportedly ahistorical, is at its core historical." Theodor Adorno, *Aesthetic Theory*, trans. and ed. Robert Hullot-Kentor (Minneapolis: University of Minnesota Press, 1997), 65.

79. William Van Orman Quine, "Identity, Ostension, and Hypostasis," *Journal of Philosophy* 48, no. 22 (October 1950): 621–633 (621–622).

80. *OS*, 63.

81. "Laws of Variation," in *OS*, 108–139.

82. See Richard Dawkins, *The View from Mount Improbable* (Harmondsworth: Penguin, 2005); *AT*, 602.

83. Pallab Ghosh, "Gene Therapy 'Aids Youth's Sight,'" *BBC News*, April 28, 2008, news.bbc.co.uk/1/hi/health/7369740.stm.

84. *AT*, 190; *EP*, 175.

85. *DDI*, 98–100.

86. *DM*, 30–32.

87. *DM*, 32–34.

88. Darwin, *Expression*, 87 (Erkman's note).

89. Pierre Teilhard de Chardin, *The Phenomenon of Man* (London: Harper Perennial, 1975). *AT* travels backward "toward" common ancestors (or "concestors"). Stephen Jay Gould argued that if one were to "wind back and play the tape" of evolution forward again, humans wouldn't necessarily appear. This isn't as strange as it may seem. See *DDI*, 300, 305–307, 321.

90. *EP*, 30.

91. The most ruthless discussion is John Carey, *What Good Are the Arts?* (London: Faber and Faber, 2005).

92. Quoted in *DDI*, 62. See Gillian Beer in *OS*, xxvii–xviii.

93. Samuel Taylor Coleridge, *Coleridge's Poetry and Prose*, ed. Nicholas Halmi, Paul Magnuson, and Raimona Modiano (New York: Norton, 2004).

94. I base my argument about "thereness" on Levinas, *Existence and Existents*, 51–60.

95. *DM*, 687.

96. Two prominent recent theorists of "coexistentialism" are Levinas and Luce Irigaray. See *TI*; Luce Irigaray, *The Way of Love*, trans. Heidi Bostic and Stephen Pluhácek (London: Continuum, 2002).

97. I support a Levinasian reading of Coleridge's poem. Though Life-in-Death is a misogynist image, there is an aspect that might help the ecological thought.

This aspect is the femininity of the face, in its horrifying combination of cosmetics and rotten flesh. This femininity is weakness and vulnerability, and it is this that the Mariner cannot face. See my analysis on the Romantic Circles blog, in particular rc.umd.edu/blog_rc/?m=200808 and rc.umd.edu/blog_rc/?m=200807.

98. See *TI*, 37, 88.

99. This poem, along with Coleridge's *The Rime of the Ancient Mariner*, is from Wordsworth and Coleridge's radical collection, *Lyrical Ballads*.

100. The most powerful writing on this aspect of the poem, and its ecological and philosophical, not to mention political, ramifications, is Marjorie Levinson, "Romantic Criticism: The State of the Art," in *At the Limits of Romanticism: Essays in Cultural, Feminist, and Materialist Criticism*, ed. Mary Favret and Nicola Watson (Bloomington: Indiana University Press, 1994), 269–281.

101. *OB*, 18.

102. "Strange distortion" is Shelley's phrase for the emergence of Rousseau as if from a tree root in *The Triumph of Life* (183). *Shelley's Poetry and Prose*, ed. Donald H. Reiman and Neil Fraistat (New York: Norton, 2002).

103. John Clare, *Major Works*, ed. Eric Robinson and David Powell, intro. by Tom Paulin (Oxford: Oxford University Press, 2004).

104. "Sexpools" are holes full of water formed during the cutting of turf.

105. Rem Koolhaas, "Junkspace," *October* 100 (Spring 2002): 175–190.

106. *TI*, 130–132 (131), 141–142.

107. *TI*, 132.

108. *TI*, 74.

109. *TI*, 139.

110. *EP*, 200, 233–234; *AT*, 193–198.

111. *OS*, 194.

112. Georges Bataille, "Animality," in *Animal Philosophy*, ed. Atterton and Calarco, 32–36 (34).

113. Sigmund Freud, "The Uncanny," in *The Standard Edition of the Complete Psychological Works of Sigmund Freud*, ed. and trans. James Strachey (London: Hogarth Press, 1953), 17:218–252 (237).

114. Section 1 of Levinas's *TI* is strong on this (33–105).

115. *AT*, 551.

116. *AT*, 552.

117. The Cure, "A Forest," *Seventeen Seconds* (Elektra/Asylum, 1980).

118. Christopher Bollas defines "normosis" as the opposite of psychosis. In psychosis, there is only the inner life; in normosis, the inner life has been evacuated. *The Shadow of the Object: Psychoanalysis of the Unthought Known* (London: Free Association Press, 1996), 135–156. Modern life codes for normosis.

119. See Clara Van Zanten, "John Ashbery and the Weather of History" (PhD diss., University of California, Davis, 2010).

120. Gilles Deleuze, *The Fold: Leibniz and the Baroque*, trans. Tom Conley (Minneapolis: University of Minnesota Press, 1993), 5.

121. See Timothy Morton, "Waste of Time," ecologywithoutnature.blogspot.com/2009/06/waste-of-time.html.

122. Timothy Morton, "Fiddlers on the Roof," ecologywithoutnature.blogspot
.com/2009/03/fiddlers-on-roof.html.

123. Timothy Morton, *The Poetics of Spice: Romantic Consumerism and the Exotic*
(Cambridge: Cambridge University Press, 2000), 105–106.

124. Timothy Morton, "Environmentalism," in *Romanticism: An Oxford Guide*,
ed. Nicholas Roe (Oxford: Oxford University Press, 2005), 696–707 (699); Morton,
The Poetics of Spice, 8–9, 32, 51–55, 104.

125. Kim Stanley Robinson, *Green Mars* (New York: Bantam, 1994), 3.

126. Martin Heidegger, "The Origin of the Work of Art," in *Poetry, Language, Thought*, trans. Albert Hofstadter (New York: Harper & Row, 1971),
15–87 (26).

2. DARK THOUGHTS

1. See *EwN*, 181–197.

2. Stanley Kubrick, Dir., *2001: A Space Odyssey* (MGM, 1968).

3. *OS*, 5.

4. *EP*, 59–60.

5. *AT*, 218.

6. *OS*, 51.

7. *OS*, 53.

8. *AT*, 266–267.

9. *OS*, 141.

10. *OS*, 251.

11. *OS*, 100.

12. Derrida only left a few tantalizing phrases about Darwin. Colin Milburn,
"Monsters in Eden: Darwin and Derrida," *Modern Language Notes* 118 (2003):
603–621.

13. See, for example, Felipe Fernández-Armesto, *So You Think You're Human?
A Brief History of Humankind* (Oxford: Oxford University Press, 2004), 4.

14. See *DDI*, 266.

15. *OS*, 34; Gillian Beer, Introduction, *OS*, xix.

16. *OS*, 163.

17. *AT*, 309–313.

18. *AT*, 316–317.

19. See *AT*, 319–320. Dawkins admits as much but is wary of the conclusion.

20. *OS*, 34–35.

21. William Van Orman Quine, "Identity, Ostension, and Hypostasis," *Journal of Philosophy* 48:22 (October 1950): 621–633 (621–622).

22. *OS*, 44. Darwin calls this the problem of "incipient species."

23. *DDI*, 100.

24. *OS*, 9.

25. *OS* 109, 131, 133.

26. *OS*, 94.

27. *DDI*, 281.

28. *AT*, 405.

29. *AT*, 406.

30. *OS*, 352; see also 162–163.

31. *OS*, 387.

32. *OS*, 351. Darwin's observation contradicts the beliefs of the Nature Philosophers, such as Oken. Paradoxically, protoplasm or *Urschleim* is the substance of idealism. See Slavoj Žižek, *In Defense of Lost Causes* (London: Verso, 2008), 444, 452.

33. *AT*, 325–329.

34. *OS*, 364.

35. *OS*, 367.

36. Sigmund Freud, "A Note upon the Mystic Writing Pad," in *The Standard Edition of the Complete Psychological Works of Sigmund Freud*, ed. and trans. James Strachey (London: Hogarth, 1953), 9:225–232. See Jacques Derrida, "Freud and the Scene of Writing," *Writing and Difference*, trans. Alan Bass (London: Routledge and Kegan Paul, 1978), 196–231.

37. Charles Darwin, *The Expression of the Emotions in Man and Animals*, intro., afterword, and commentary by Paul Erkman (London: Harper Collins, 1999); *AT*, 197.

38. See *OS*, 259.

39. *OS*, 160.

40. *OS*, 165.

41. *OS*, 164–165.

42. See *OB*, 23, 42. "Monstration" doesn't exactly oppose Levinas's "face," because then a metaphysical inside–outside distinction would arise. See Jean Greisch, "The Face and Reading: Immediacy and Mediation," in *Re-Reading Levinas*, ed. Robert Berlasconi and Simon Critchley (Bloomington: Indiana University Press, 1991), 67–82 (77).

43. See *OS*, 43.

44. *OS*, 102.

45. *OS*, 94.

46. *OS*, 93.

47. *OS*, 105–106.

48. *OED*, "chimera," n. 2: "A grotesque monster, formed of the parts of various animals." The word has various biological definitions: see also n. 3.d.: "An organism (commonly a plant) in which tissues of genetically different constitution coexist as a result of grafting, mutation, or some other process." The dictionary cites a 1968 issue of *Nature*: "Mouse chimaeras obtained by the injection of cells into the blastocyst." See *DDI*, 286–288. See also Jacques Derrida, *The Animal That Therefore I Am*, ed. Marie-Louise Mallet, trans. David Wills (New York: Fordham University Press, 2008), 23, 41–47.

49. *OS*, 161.

50. *OS*, 40.

51. *OS*, 40, 41.

52. *AT*, 530; see also 312–313.

53. *EP*, 156.

54. See Slavoj Žižek, *The Indivisible Remainder: An Essay on Schelling and Related Matters* (London: Verso, 1996). This idea is related to Deleuze's reworking of Spinoza, who proved that matter moves of its own accord.

55. *AT*, 582–594.

56. This is the view of Graham Cairns-Smith. See *DDI*, 157–158 (the quotation comes from 205); *AT*, 581–582.

57. Douglas Hofstadter, *Gödel, Escher, Bach: An Eternal Golden Braid* (New York: Basic Books, 1999), 541–543. The viral sentence (known as a Henkin sentence) sounds amazingly like Lacan's "il y a de l'un."

58. Przemyslaw Prusinkiewicz and Aristid Lindenmayer, *The Algorithmic Beauty of Plants*, with James S. Hanan, F. David Fracchia, Deborah Fowler, Martin J. M. de Boer, and Lynn Mercer (Przemyslaw Prusinkiewicz, 2004), available at algorithmicbotany.org/papers/.

59. *AT*, 273–275.

60. *OS*, 68.

61. *DM*, 444–451.

62. *DM*, 449.

63. *DM*, 449–450.

64. J. David Smith, "The Study of Animal Metacognition," *Trends in Cognitive Sciences* 13, no. 9 (September, 2009): 389–396.

65. *DM*, 89, 92–93, 95–96.

66. *DM*, 408.

67. *DM*, 151.

68. We share this with chimps. See *DDI*, 379–380.

69. Fernández-Armesto, *So You Think You're Human?* 54.

70. *DM*, 375.

71. Alan M. Turing, "Computing Machinery and Intelligence," in *PAI*, 40–66.

72. Hofstadter, *Gödel, Escher, Bach*, 680.

73. See, for example, *DM*, 244, 246. See also John Bellamy Foster, *Marx's Ecology: Materialism and Nature* (New York: Monthly Review Press, 2000).

74. Arthur Schopenhauer, *The World as Will and Representation*, trans. E. F. J. Payne, 2 vols. (New York: Dover Publications, 1969), 1.88–91, 1.249.

75. Francisco Varela, Evan Thompson, and Eleanor Rosch, *The Embodied Mind: Cognitive Science and Human Experience* (Cambridge, MA: MIT Press, 1992), 208–211.

76. Turing, "Computing Machinery and Intelligence," 55.

77. John Searle, "Minds, Brains, and Programs," in *PAI*, 67–88 (78, 79–80); Margaret A. Boden, "Escaping from the Chinese Room," in *PAI*, 89–104 (100).

78. See *DDI*, 205–207.

79. See *DDI*, 370.

80. *AT*, 406.

81. *AT*, 484–485.

82. Karl Marx, *Capital*, trans. Ben Fowkes (Harmondsworth: Penguin, 1990), 1.284.

83. Searle, "Minds, Brains, and Programs," 80.

84. Stanley Kubrick, dir., *The Shining* (Hawk Films, 1976).

85. See Malcolm Bull, "Where Is the Anti-Nietzsche?" *New Left Review* 3, 2nd ser. (May–June 2000): 121–145.

86. Jacques Lacan, *Le seminaire, Livre III: Les psychoses* (Paris: Editions de Seuil, 1981), 48. See Slavoj Žižek, *The Parallax View* (Cambridge, MA: MIT Press, 2006), 206.

87. *DM*, 211.

88. *OS*, 335.

89. *OED*, "chimera," n. 3.b.

90. Werner Herzog, dir., *Grizzly Man* (Discovery Docs, 2005).

91. Judy Irving, dir., *The Wild Parrots of Telegraph Hill* (Pelican Media, 2003).

92. Arne Naess, *Ecology, Community, and Lifestyle: Outline of an Ecosophy* (Cambridge: Cambridge University Press, 1989), 74.

93. Gilles Deleuze, *The Fold: Leibniz and the Baroque*, trans. Tom Conley (Minneapolis: University of Minnesota Press, 1993), 5.

94. William Blake, *The Complete Poetry and Prose of William Blake*, ed. D. V. Erdman (New York: Doubleday, 1988).

95. Georg Wilhelm Freidrich Hegel, "Jenaer Realphilosophie," in *Fruehe politische Systeme*, ed. Gerhard Göhler (Frankfurt: Ullstein, 1974), 201–289 (204).

96. George Morrison, *The Weaving of Glory* (Grand Rapids, MI: Kregel Publications, 1994), 106.

97. Steven Spielberg, dir., *AI* (Warner Brothers, 2001).

98. Jonathan Frakes, dir., *Star Trek: First Contact* (Paramount Pictures, 1996).

99. *The Prelude* 5.557–591. William Wordsworth, *The Major Works: Including the Prelude*, ed. Stephen Gill (Oxford: Oxford University Press, 2008).

100. This idea is part of Derrida's concept of *différance* and of Wolfgang Iser's literary theory: see Wolfgang Iser, *The Implied Reader: Patterns of Communication in Prose Fiction from Bunyan to Beckett* (Baltimore: Johns Hopkins University Press, 1974), 33.

101. Wolfgang Iser, *The Act of Reading: A Theory of Aesthetic Response* (Baltimore: Johns Hopkins University Press, 1978), 206–207.

102. Jean-Paul Sartre, *Being and Nothingness: An Essay on Phenomenological Ontology*, trans. and ed. Hazel Barnes (New York: The Philosophical Library, 1969), 341–347 (343).

103. *TI*, 25–27, 51, 62, 80, 150–151, 170–171, 199, 207, 258–259, 290–292. The Dalai Lama concurs ("others are infinity"): "Universal Responsibility in the Modern World," Royal Albert Hall, London, May 22, 2008; see furhhdl.org.

104. Georges Bataille: "The animal opens before me a depth that attracts me and is familiar to me." "Animality," in *Animal Philosophy: Ethics and Identity*, ed. Peter Atterton and Matthew Calarco (London: Continuum, 2007), 32–36 (35). *TI*

is a landmark of investigation. Mutual recognition is a vital part of the ethics of Georg Wilhelm Friedrich Hegel's *Hegel's Phenomenology of Spirit*, trans. A. V. Miller, analysis and foreword by J. N. Findlay (Oxford: Oxford University Press, 1977), 110.

105. Luce Irigaray, "Animal Compassion," in *Animal Philosophy*, ed. Atterton and Calarco, 195–201 (201).

106. See Jean-François Lyotard, *Peregrinations: Law, Form, Event* (New York: Columbia University Press, 1988), 5; *The Inhuman: Reflections on Time*, trans. Geoffrey Bennington and Rachel Bowlby (Oxford: Blackwell, 1991), 19.

107. Turing, "Computing Machinery and Intelligence."

108. See David Mitchell and Sharon Snyder, "Narrative Prosthesis and the Materiality of Metaphor," in *The Disability Studies Reader*, ed. Lennard Davis (London: Routledge, 2006), 205–217; "Compulsory Able-Bodiedness and Queer/Disabled Existence," in ibid., 301–308.

109. Hegel, "Jenaer Realphilosophie," 204.

110. See *TI*, 158.

111. *TI*, 170.

112. *TI*, 199.

113. See Judith Butler, *Gender Trouble: Feminism and the Subversion of Identity* (London: Routledge, 1990).

114. *EP*, 156.

115. Scott LaFee, "Online-World Immersion Probes 'Possibilities of Transformation.'" *The San Diego Union-Tribune*, December 12, 2008, signonsandiego .com/stories/2008/dec/21/1a21virtual162313-online-world-immersion-probes-po/ ?uniontrib.

116. Jon Krakauer, *Into the Wild* (New York: Anchor, 2007). Sean Penn, dir., *Into the Wild* (Paramount Vantage, 2007).

117. See *TI*, 192–193, 200.

118. Joan Roughgarden, *Evolution's Rainbow: Diversity, Gender, and Sexuality in Nature and People* (Berkeley: University of California Press, 2004), 27, 34–35.

119. Ibid., 36.

120. Claude Nuridsany and Marie Pérennou, dirs., *Microcosmos: Le peuple de l'herbe* (Agencie Jules Verne, 1997); *DM*, 303–304.

121. *OS*, 76–79; *DM*, 257.

122. *AT*, 626.

123. *EP*, 160.

124. *EP*, 156; Roughgarden, *Evolution's Rainbow*, 26–27.

125. *EP*, 263–264.

126. Hofstadter, *Gödel, Escher, Bach*, 360–361, 613–614.

127. For further discussion of speciesism, see Cary Wolfe, *Animal Rites: American Culture, the Discourse of Species, and Posthumanist Theory* (Chicago: University of Chicago Press, 2003), 33–38.

128. *DM*, 188–189.

129. *DM*, 191.

130. *DM*, 189.

131. See Gilles Deleuze and Félix Guattari, "1914: One or Several Wolves?" in *A Thousand Plateaus: Capitalism and Schizophrenia*, trans. Brian Massumi (Minneapolis: University of Minnesota Press, 1987), 26–38. Donna Haraway harries them in *When Species Meet* (Minneapolis: University of Minnesota Press, 2007).

132. See Donna Haraway, *The Companion Species Manifesto: Dogs, People, and Significant Otherness* (Chicago: Prickly Paradigm Press, 2003).

133. See G. J. Barker Benfield, *The Culture of Sensibility: Sex and Society in Eighteenth-Century Britain* (Chicago: University of Chicago Press, 1992).

134. Andrew Stanton, dir., *Wall • E* (Pixar Animation Studios, 2008).

135. See Anne-Lise François, "'O Happy Living Things': Frankenfoods and the Bounds of Wordsworthian Natural Piety," *diacritics* 33, no. 2 (Summer 2003): 42–70.

136. *Wo Es war, soll Ich werden* (Where Id was, there shall Ego be). Sigmund Freud, Lecture 31, "The Dissection of the Psychical Personality," *New Introductory Lectures on Psycho-Analysis* (New York: Norton, 1989), 71–100 (99–100).

137. Timothy Morton, *The Poetics of Spice: Romantic Consumerism and the Exotic* (Cambridge: Cambridge University Press, 2000), 8–9. Fernand Braudel, *The Perspective of the World: Vol. 3. Civilization and Capitalism* (New York: Harper & Row, 1984).

138. Arthur Rimbaud, letter to Paul Demeny, May 15, 1871, in *Rimbaud: Complete Works, Selected Letters: A Bilingual Edition*, ed. Seth Whidden, trans. Wallace Fowlie (Chicago: University of Chicago Press, 2005), 374.

139. Percy Shelley, *Shelley's Poetry and Prose*, ed. Donald H. Reiman and Neil Fraistat (New York: Norton, 2002).

140. Daniel C. Dennett, "Cognitive Wheels: The Frame Problem of AI," in *PAI*, 147–170 (158).

141. "Neanderthals Speak Again after 30,000 Years," *ScienceDaily*, April 21, 2008, sciencedaily.com/releases/2008/04/080421154426.htm.

142. See Fernández-Armesto, *So You Think You're Human?* 129–130.

143. Steven Mithen, "The Evolution of Imagination: An Archaeological Perspective," *SubStance* 94/95 (2001): 28–54 (43–44). For a counterargument, see Fernández-Armesto, *So You Think You're Human?* 24, 135.

144. "'Complexity' of Neanderthal Tools," *BBC News*, August 26, 2008, news .bbc.co.uk/1/hi/sci/tech/7582912.stm.

145. Fernández-Armesto, *So You Think You're Human?* 132–133.

146. Herbert A. Simon, *The Sciences of the Artificial* (Cambridge, MA: MIT Press, 1996), 51–53.

147. Hubert L. Dreyfus and Stuart E. Dreyfus, "Making a Mind versus Modeling the Brain: Artificial Intelligence Back at a Branch-Point," in *PAI*, 309–333 (328); some AI research approaches the assertion that we can program prejudice, such as a sense of family and nationality (328–329)—who knew?

148. Ibid., 328, 331.

149. Fernández-Armesto, *So You Think You're Human?* 65.

150. See Jared Diamond, *The Third Chimpanzee* (New York: Harper Perennial, 2006).

151. Mike Scully, "Beyond Blunderdome," *The Simpsons*, dir. Steven Dean Moore (Fox, September 26, 1999).

152. *DM*, 210.

153. *AT*, 469.

154. William Golding, *The Inheritors* (New York: Harcourt, Brace, and World, 1955), 223–233.

155. Jean M. Auel, *The Clan of the Cave Bear* (New York: Bantam, 2002).

156. Like "Old Man Travelling," "The Idiot Boy" first appeared in Wordsworth and Coleridge's radical, experimental collection, *Lyrical Ballads*. My discussion is informed by Avital Ronell, *Stupidity* (Urbana: University of Illinois Press, 2002).

157. *DM*, 100; *OS*, 169.

158. Ronell, *Stupidity*, 252–253.

159. The decisive study is David Simpson, *Wordsworth, Commodification, and Social Concern: The Poetics of Modernity* (Cambridge: Cambridge University Press, 2009).

160. For a compelling discussion of the *Müsselman*, see Slavoj Žižek, "Neighbors and Other Monsters: A Plea for Ethical Violence," in Slavoj Žižek, Eric L. Santner, and Kenneth Reinhard, *The Neighbor: Three Inquiries in Political Theology* (Chicago: University of Chicago Press, 2006), 134–190; and David Simpson, *9/11: The Culture of Commemoration* (Chicago: University of Chicago Press, 2006), 162–165.

161. George W. Bush, Presidential Debate, October 3, 2000, debates.org/pages/trans2000a.html.

162. *OED*, "render," v.IV.17.a.

163. Stephen Foster, *Stephen Foster Songbook*, ed. Richard Jackson (New York: Dover, 1974).

164. Samuel Taylor Coleridge, *Coleridge's Poetry and Prose*, ed. Nicholas Halmi, Paul Magnuson, and Raimona Modiano (New York: Norton, 2004).

165. I disagree with Gregory Bateson here: Gregory Bateson and Mary Catherine Bateson, *Angels Fear: Towards an Epistemology of the Sacred* (New York: Macmillan, 1987), 76.

166. See Jacques Derrida, "Economimesis," *Diacritics* 11, no. 2 (Summer 1981): 2–25; Captain Beefheart and His Magic Band, "Pena," *Trout Mask Replica* (Straight Records, 1969).

167. For fireworks as an aesthetic mode, see Theodor Adorno, *Aesthetic Theory*, trans. and ed. Robert Hullot-Kentor (Minneapolis: University of Minnesota Press, 1997), 81.

168. See *OB*, 15, 48, 55, 75, 92–93, 113–115; see Thomas Carl Wall, *Radical Passivity: Levinas, Balchot, and Agamben* (Albany: State University of New York Press, 1999), 31–64.

169. See Walter Benjamin, *The Origin of German Tragic Drama*. (London: NLB, 1977), 200–233.

170. See Stephen Crawford, "On Freud's 'Mourning and Melancholia,'" talk given to the Islington Churches Bereavement Service, London (n.d.).

171. See Judith Butler, "Melancholy Gender / Refused Identification," in *The Psychic Life of Power: Theories in Subjection* (Stanford, CA: Stanford University Press, 1997), 132–50; see esp. 4, 138–40; Timothy Morton, "Queer Ecology," *PMLA* (forthcoming).

172. See Erich Fromm, *To Have or to Be?* (London: Continuum, 2007), 160.

173. René Descartes, *Meditations and Other Metaphysical Writings*, trans. and intro. by Desmond M. Clarke (Harmondsworth: Penguin, 1998, 2000), 19.

174. Immanuel Kant, *Critique of Judgment*, trans. Werner S. Pluhar (Indianapolis: Hackett, 1987), 113.

175. See *TI*, 217–218.

176. *OS*, 198.

177. See Slavoj Žižek in Sophie Fiennes, dir., *The Pervert's Guide to Cinema* (Amoeba Film, Kasander Film Company, Lone Star Productions, Mischief Films, 2006).

3. FORWARD THINKING

1. Rachel Carson, *Silent Spring*, intro. by Linda Lear, afterword by E. O. Wilson (Boston: Houghton Mifflin, 2002).

2. Gregory Bateson and Mary Catherine Bateson, *Angels Fear: Towards an Epistemology of the Sacred* (New York: Macmillan, 1987), 76.

3. Emmanuel Levinas, interview with François Poirié, in *Is It Righteous to Be? Interviews with Emmanuel Levinas*, ed. Jill Robbins (Stanford, CA: Stanford University Press, 2001), 23–83 (49).

4. For example, see James Lovelock, *The Revenge of Gaia: Earth's Climate Crisis and the Fate of Humanity* (New York: Basic Books, 2007).

5. See Slavoj Žižek, *Parallax View* (London: Verso, 2005) 17–18.

6. Karl Marx, *Capital*, trans. Ben Fowkes (Harmondsworth: Penguin, 1990), 1.452–453. See also Fredric Jameson, "Notes on Globalization as a Philosophical Issue," in *The Cultures of Globalization*, ed. Fredric Jameson and Masao Miyoshi (Durham, NC: Duke University Press, 1997), 54–79.

7. *EwN*, 122–123.

8. U.S.A. for Africa, "We Are the World" (Columbia, 1985).

9. Fredric Jameson, *Postmodernism, or, The Cultural Logic of Late Capitalism* (Durham, NC: Duke University Press, 1991).

10. For "full spectrum dominance," see Rahul Mahajan, *Full Spectrum Dominance: U.S. Power in Iraq and Beyond* (New York: Seven Stories Press, 2003).

11. Laurie Anderson, "O Superman," *Big Science* (Warner Bros., 1982).

12. See *EwN*, 29–78.

13. Talking Heads, "The Overload," *Remain in Light* (Sire Records, 1980).

14. Keith Rowe quoted in David Toop, *Haunted Weather: Music, Silence, and Memory* (London: Serpent's Tail, 2004), 239–240.

15. Julia Kristeva has explored the relationship between the "genotext" and the "phenotext": "[Genotext] will include semiotic processes but also the

advent of the symbolic. The former includes drives, their disposition and their division of the body, plus the ecological and social system surrounding the body, such as objects and pre-Oedipal relations with parents. The latter encompasses the emergence of object and subject, and the constitution of nuclei of meaning involving categories: semantic and categorical fields"; see *Revolution in Poetic Language*, trans. Margaret Waller, in *The Kristeva Reader*, ed. Toril Moi (Oxford: Blackwell, 1986), 89–136 (120). We could argue that ambience was the "extended phenotext." This is appropriate, since the genotext includes the ecosystem.

16. See, for example, Bill McKibben, interview in *Elephant*, Summer 2007, 56.

17. Percy Shelley, *A Defence of Poetry*, in *Shelley's Poetry and Prose*, ed. Donald H. Reiman and Neil Fraistat (New York: Norton, 2002), 535.

18. See Timothy Morton, "The Dark Ecology of Elegy," in *The Oxford Handbook of the Elegy*, ed. Karen Weisman (Oxford: Oxford University Press, forthcoming).

19. Peter Sacks, *The English Elegy: Studies in the Genre from Spenser to Yeats* (Baltimore: Johns Hopkins University Press, 1985), 24–25.

20. I borrow the phrase "happy-happy-joy-joy" from "Stimpy's Invention," an episode of John Kricfalusi's *The Ren and Stimpy Show* (Games Animation; Nickelodeon, 1991–1996).

21. This is Giorgio Agamben's phrase, found in *The Coming Community*, trans. Michael Hardt (Minneapolis: University of Minnesota Press, 2007), 49.

22. See Walter Benjamin, "The Work of Art in the Age of Mechanical Reproduction," in *Illuminations*, ed. Hannah Arendt, trans. Harry Zohn (London: Harcourt, Brace and World, 1973), 217–251 (222–223).

23. "Unworking" is Scott Shershow's translation of *désoeuvrement:* see *The Work and the Gift* (Chicago: University of Chicago Press, 2005), 193–205; Jean-Luc Nancy, *The Inoperative Community*, trans. Peter Connor et al. (Minneapolis: University of Minnesota Press, 1991).

24. For diastic poetry, see eskimo.com/~rstarr/poormfa/diastic.html.

25. Benoit Mandelbrot, *The Fractal Geometry of Nature* (New York: W.H. Freeman, 1983).

26. *EwN*, 96.

27. Guy Debord, "Theory of the *Derive*," library.nothingness.org/articles/all/en/display/314.

28. Virginia Woolf, *Mrs. Dalloway* (London: Hogarth Press, 1990), 27–28.

29. Virginia Woolf, *To the Lighthouse*, ed. Margaret Drabble (Oxford: Oxford University Press, 2000), 169–194.

30. See jacketmagazine.com/12/bergvall.html.

31. Sadly, much of La Monte Young's catalog is currently out of print, but you can learn about it at melafoundation.org/main.htm.

32. A good example is Eliane Radigue, *L'Ile re-sonante* (Shiiin, 2005).

33. See, for example, Alvin Lucier, *I Am Sitting in a Room* (Lovely Music, 1990); see *EwN*, 47–48.

34. Barry Cleveland, "In Search of the Uncommon Chord," *Guitar Player*, April 2008, 74–88.

35. I offer the following all too brief selection of Allan Holdsworth's work: UK, *UK* (E.G. Records, 1978); Allan Holdsworth, *The Sixteen Men of Tain* (Globe Music Media, 2003); and *Then!* (Alternity Records, 2004).

36. Robin Mackay, "Dark Ecologies: Paul Chaney at Goldfish Contemporary Art," review of Paul Chaney, "The Lonely Now," at Goldfish Contemporary Art, Penzance (UK), 2008, artcornwall.org/features/paul_chaney_robin_mackay.htm; Paul Chaney, *The Lonely Now* (Goldfish, 2008).

37. Comora Tolliver, "Pod," Cranbrook Academy of Art, 2007–.

38. See John Seabrook, "Sowing for Apocalypse: The Quest for a Global Seed Bank," *The New Yorker*, August 27, 2007, 60–71.

39. See comoratolliver.com/installation.html.

40. See Timothy Morton, "Ecologocentrism: Unworking Animals," *SubStance* 37, no. 3 (2008): 37–61.

41. Andrei Tarkovsky, dir., *Solaris* (Mosfilm, 1972).

42. See Roger Penrose, *The Emperor's New Mind: Concerning Computers, Minds, and the Laws of Physics* (Oxford: Oxford University Press, 1989, 1990), 126.

43. I refer to the 1960s television series *The Prisoner*.

44. See Žižek, *Parallax View*, 181–182.

45. Ridley Scott, dir., *Blade Runner* (Blade Runner Partnership, The Ladd Company, Run Run Shaw, The Shaw Brothers, 1982).

46. Mary Shelley, *Frankenstein*, ed. Maurice Hindle (Harmondsworth: Penguin, 2003), 225.

47. See Slavoj Žižek's masterful "I or He or It (the Thing) Which Thinks," in *Tarrying with the Negative: Kant, Hegel, and the Critique of Ideology* (Durham, NC: Duke University Press, 1993), 10–44.

48. Mary Shelley succumbed to this interpretation herself in the preface to the 1831 edition: *Frankenstein*, 5–10.

49. Derek Parfit, *Reasons and Persons* (Oxford: Oxford University Press, 1982), 199–201.

50. *OB*, 116.

51. See, for example, N. Katherine Hayles, *How We Became Posthuman: Virtual Bodies in Cybernetics, Literature, and Informatics* (Chicago: University of Chicago Press, 1999); Hubert L. Dreyfus and Stuart E. Dreyfus, "Making a Mind versus Modeling the Brain: Artificial Intelligence Back at a Branch-Point," in *PAI*, 309–333 (309, 315).

52. *OB*, 128.

53. *DDI*, 471.

54. Slavoj Žižek, "Neighbors and Other Monsters: A Plea for Ethical Violence," in *The Neighbor: Three Inquiries in Political Theology*, ed. Slavoj Žižek, Eric Santner, and Kenneth Reinhard (Chicago: University of Chicago Press, 2005), 134–190 (159–160).

55. See, in particular, *TI*, 197–198.

56. Jacques Derrida, *The Animal That Therefore I Am*, ed. Marie-Louise Mallet, trans. David Wills (New York: Fordham University Press, 2008), 95.

57. Douglas Hofstader, *Gödel, Escher, Bach: An Eternal Golden Braid* (New York: Basic Books, 1999), 707.

58. See Stephen Mulhall, "Marketplace Atheism," review of Owen Flanagan, *The Problem of the Soul*, London Review of Books 11 (September 2003): 28–29 (28).

59. Gary Marcus, *Kluge: The Haphazard Evolution of the Human Mind* (New York: Houghton Mifflin, 2008).

60. See Andy Clark, "Connectionism, Competence, and Explanation," in *PAI*, 281–308 (305, 296–297).

61. See Agamben, *Coming Community*, 93; *The Open: Man and Animal*, trans. Kevin Attell (Stanford, CA: Stanford University Press, 2004), 39–43.

62. Martin Heidegger, "The Origin of the Work of Art," in *Poetry, Language, Thought*, trans. Albert Hofstadter (New York: Harper & Row, 1971), 45. Derrida has commented extensively on Heidegger's idea that animals are poor in world (*Weltarm*): *Of Spirit: Heidegger and the Question*, trans. Geoffrey Bennington and Rachel Bowlby (Chicago: University of Chicago Press, 1991), 47–57; "'Eating Well', or, The Calculation of the Subject," in Jacques Derrida, *Points: Interviews, 1974–1994* (Stanford: Stanford University Press, 1995), 255–287 (277); Derrida, *The Animal That Therefore I Am*, 141–160.

63. Francisco Varela, Evan Thompson, and Eleanor Rosch, *The Embodied Mind: Cognitive Science and Human Experience* (Cambridge, MA: MIT Press, 1992), 90, 152.

64. Žižek, *Parallax View*, 163. See Luce Irigaray, *The Way of Love*, trans. Heidi Bostic and Stephen Pluhácek (London: Continuum, 2002), 120. Derrida goes so far as to claim that Darwin provides the greatest humiliation: *The Animal That Therefore I Am*, 136.

65. See *DDI*, 100.

66. *AT*, 569–570.

67. Irigaray, *The Way of Love*, 91.

68. See Derek Parfit, "Experiences, Subjects, and Conceptual Schemes," *Philosophical Topics* 26, no. 1–2 (Spring and Fall, 1999): 217–270.

69. *EP*, 187–191.

70. Levinas is thus a scientific realist: see *OB*, xxiii.

71. *DDI*, 498–499.

72. There is some marvelous deconstructive thinking on this in David Wood, *The Step Back: Ethics and Politics after Deconstruction* (Albany: State University of New York Press, 2005), 172–173; and Timothy Clark, "Towards a Deconstructive Environmental Criticism," *Oxford Literary Review* 30, no. 1 (2008): 45–68.

73. Terry Gilliam, dir., *Twelve Monkeys* (Atlas Entertainment, 1995).

74. Garrett Hardin, "The Tragedy of the Commons," *Science*, December 13, 1968, 1243–1248.

75. Timothy Morton, *The Poetics of Spice: Romantic Consumerism and the Exotic* (Cambridge: Cambridge University Press, 2000), 59, 104, 11, 214–215.

76. Derek Parfit, *Reasons and Persons* (Oxford: Oxford University Press, 1984), 384–390, 419–441 (432–433).

77. John Vucetich and Michael Nelson, "Abandon Hope: Live Sustainably Just Because It's the Right Thing to Do," *The Ecologist* 39, no. 2 (March 2009): 32–35.

78. *EwN*, 135–43.

79. See *EwN*, 100–101.

80. I am thinking in particular of Derrida's *The Animal That Therefore I Am*, 3–11.

81. Felipe Fernández-Armesto, *So You Think You're Human? A Brief History of Humankind* (Oxford: Oxford University Press, 2004), 48.

82. Ibid., 51.

83. Levinas approaches something like this in *TI*, 37, 88. See *DDI*, 426.

84. See *DDI*, 426.

85. *DDI*, 486.

86. See Žižek, *In Defense of Lost Causes* (London: Verso, 2008), 446–447.

87. See Bruno Latour, *Politics of Nature: How to Bring the Sciences into Democracy* (Cambridge, MA: Harvard University Press, 2004).

88. Agamben, *Coming Community*, 32, 86–87. Agamben stresses absolute potentiality, symbolized by the image of the tabula rasa (37).

89. Erich Fromm, *To Have or to Be?* (London: Continuum, 2007), 35.

90. See *TI*, 37–38. See also Levinas, interview with François Poirié, in *Is It Righteous to Be?* 53. The Pascal quotation forms one of the epigraphs to *OB* (vii).

91. Irigaray, *The Way of Love*, 77.

92. Agamben, *Coming Community*, 65.

93. See Fromm, *To Have or to Be?* 79.

94. *TI*, 39, 80.

95. Thomas Carl Wall, *Radical Passivity: Levinas, Blanchot, and Agamben* (New York: State University of New York Press, 1999), 1–12.

96. Agamben, *Coming Community*, 103.

97. See Fromm, *To Have or to Be?* 164.

98. Irigaray's *The Way of Love* explores this theme. See especially 36, 47–49, 51–53, 115. Irigaray is one of the few "Continental" thinkers prepared to acknowledge biological continuity, for example, in the form of the mother's body (74–75). Her view is rather more Romantic than mine—she prefers "another world here beside me" to "the remote verticality of other planets," whereas I see these two ideas as intertwined.

99. See *TI*, 69, 72, 89.

100. *TI*, 150, 151, 155.

101. *TI*, 179; Erich Fromm, *To Have or to Be?* 2.

102. *TI*, 150, 152–153, 163–165. Levinas puts it this way: one needs the comfort of a place to live before one can look out onto the infinite.

103. See *TI*, 179–180.

104. *TI*, 256–257 (256).

105. Emmanuel Levinas, *Existence and Existents*, trans. Alphonso Lingis (Pittsburgh: Duquesne University Press, 2003), 93.

106. *TI*, 259, 256.

107. *TI*, 259.

108. *TI*, 306.

109. See *OB*, 182.

110. Sigmund Freud, *Interpreting Dreams*, tr. J.A. Underwood (London and New York: Penguin, 2006), 131.

111. Ridley Scott, dir., *Alien* (Brandywine Productions, 1979).

112. See Slavoj Žižek, *The Sublime Object of Ideology* (London: Verso, 1991), 79.

113. Philip Merilees coined this phrase for Edward Lorenz at a meeting of the American Association for the Advancement of Science in 1972.

114. See Steven Jonson, *Emergence: The Connected Lives of Ants, Brains, Cities, and Software* (New York: Simon & Schuster, 2002).

115. *DM*, 366.

116. I am paraphrasing George Morrison, *The Weaving of Glory* (Grand Rapids, MI: Kregel Publications, 1994), 106.

117. See nonukes.org/ngl.htm.

118. U.S. Secretary of State Bill Richardson thwarted the plan in 2000. The scheme would have released six thousand tons of radioactive nickel from Oak Ridge, Tennessee, for manufacture in household items such as silverware. See energycommerce.house.gov/press/106nr7.shtml.

119. Marx, *Capital*, 556.

120. Edward Thomas, "First Known When Lost," in *The Collected Poems of Edward Thomas*, ed. R. George Thomas (Oxford: Oxford University Press, 1981). By permission of Oxford University Press.

121. See Mark Townsend and Paul Harris, "Now the Pentagon Tells Bush: Climate Change Will Destroy Us," *The Observer*, February 22, 2004, guardian.co.uk/environment/2004/feb/22/usnews.theobserver. See also Paul Virilio, *Popular Defense and Ecological Struggles*, trans. Mark Polizzotti (New York: Semiotext(e), 1990).

122. Francis Fukuyama, *The End of History and the Last Man* (New York: Free Press, 2006).

123. *Wo Es war, soll Ich werden* (Where Id was, there shall Ego be). Sigmund Freud, Lecture 31, "The Dissection of the Psychical Personality," in *New Introductory Lectures on Psycho-Analysis* (New York: Norton, 1989), 71–100 (99–100).

124. Ted Nordhaus and Michael Shellenberger, *Break Through: From the Death of Environmentalism to the Politics of Possibility* (Boston: Houghton Mifflin, 2007). See also "The Death of Environmentalism" (Ted Nordhaus and Michael Shellenberger; available online at thebreakthrough.org/images/Death_of_Environmentalism.pdf).

125. T. S. Eliot, *Collected Poems, 1909–1962* (London: Faber and Faber, 1974).

126. For further discussion, see *EwN*, 109–123.

127. Walter Benjamin, "Notes to the Theses on History," in *Gesammelte Schriften*, ed. Theodor Adorno and Gershom Scholem (Frankfurt am Main: Surkhamp, 1972), 1.1232.

128. Georges Bataille, *Theory of Religion*, trans. Robert Hurley (Cambridge, MA: MIT Press, 1992), 57.

Index